DICK CLARK'S PROGRAM FOR SUCCESS

In Your Business And Personal Life

CORNERSTONE LIBRARY

NEW YORK

Published by Cornerstone Library
A Simon & Schuster Subsidiary of
Gulf & Western Corporation
Simon & Schuster Building
1230 Avenue of the Americas
New York, New York 10020

The trademark of Cornerstone Library, Inc. consists of the words
"Cornerstone Library" and the portrayal of a cube and is registered in the
United States Patent Office

Manufactured in the United States of America

ISBN 346-12440-9

Contents

Introduction

How to Use This Book

When I sat down to write this book, I had a special motivation operating inside me. I wanted it to be more than just a run-through of my life story and an enumeration of successes. Life has not been all that easy for me, yet I have survived and thrived. The exterior view of my life would merely reveal a rapid climb to success in several aspects of the entertainment business. Even the "inside story" would fall short of telling you what I wanted you to know. A revelatory autobiography would give you the agony as well as the ecstasy but wouldn't show you how to preserve the latter in spite of the former.

This book will give you the good and the bad sides of my life. But I will go beyond recounting my history. Each lesson my life can teach is highlighted in a separate survival workshop section at the end of the book. This will help you put into action the remedies and survival tactics I have learned in my life in order to make yours easier.

In a way, that sounds like the advice offered to each of us by our parents: "Learn from my mistakes. Don't feel you have to go ahead and try something your way when I know, through my life experience, that it won't work." I really don't want to be preachy or to discourage your own experimentation as would an over-protective parent. But, my life has taught me many things about survival and success, and, if you take these things into consideration, your own experimentation in life may be less trial-and-error and more trial-and-success. I will give you the basic dance steps to survival; you'll have to put your stamp of individuality on in order to win your contest as I did to win mine.

After reading each chapter, it would be a good idea to launch right into the related exercises and tests in the Appendix while the lessons of my life are still fresh in your mind. Some people, however, will find it disconcerting to take such a detour. They might prefer to follow my story through from beginning to end. For these people, it would be wise to skip the exercises until having read the entire story. Then, after having completed the autobiographical section, you can use the Appendix as a workshop experience to improve your survival abilities.

Remember, as you read this book, that, despite my good fortune, I am really an ordinary person. I'm not trying to win you over with false modesty, I promise. I'm no more intelligent than many people and have had no better an upbringing than the average person. I'm not a Harvard graduate, and the closest I ever came to Choate was when I drove to Vermont on a ski trip via the Wilbur Cross Expressway. Yet I have succeeded by anyone's standards. The value of my story is that it is a blueprint for success and survival for ordinary people, not superstars. Whatever I have done, you can do in your life, as well!

Let my life be the workshop for yours. Let my survival lessons increase the probability of your survival and success.

1

Getting Set—
Taking Stock

"Mr. Clark, the captain would like all passengers to fasten their seat belts," the attractive stewardess said, jogging me out of some deep thinking about my forthcoming movie on the Beatles. At that moment, the gruff, matter-of-fact announcement came over the aircraft's public address system: "This is Captain Stewart. We are encountering some severe turbulence and would ask that all passengers fasten their seat belts. We'll be arriving in New York about twenty minutes behind schedule. Sorry for the delay."

Just then, the aircraft lurched violently and began to toss about like a cork on a rough sea. One woman behind me gasped. The stewardess's smile faded as she hastened to an empty seat and buckled up. We must have hit an air pocket and descended at 2,000 feet per minute.

"This wouldn't be a convenient time to die," I told myself. "I've got nineteen movie deals in the works; I've got to make the 'Variety Show' work, despite Fred Silverman's professional opposition to the concept; I've just taken over the bankrupt Westchester Premier Theater and need to turn it around; and I still need to fulfill many network obligations." In the midst of a survival crisis, I began to take stock of my outstanding chores and obligations and decided that death would have to wait a while before claiming me. I mused about making an announcement to the Angel of Death: "This is Dick Clark speaking. I've decided that I have too much work to do. Come back some other time."

I looked for something to think about as a distraction and confidence booster. I thought about the years since the beginning of my career and surveyed what I've built since then. Could I ever have expected to achieve so much back in Utica when I had just started out as a radio newscaster? I knew I was good—lots of people told me so early on in my career. But what has carried me so far, all these years, always successfully?

Playing chess flashed in my mind, as I sat there bouncing around in the airplane. "I've been a Grand Master at chess. That's it!" I realized. My approach to life—my survival secret—has been to employ the same strategy used by chess champions. Think many moves ahead; know your adversary's style of play and his psychology; be prepared to react to the unconventional challenge. An episode came to mind.

Fred Silverman and I were never the best of friends. We have mutual professional respect but frequently see issues differently. His style is to go it alone. He's a genius in his sphere or programming, and maybe that's the way he must operate. But it grates on me to see a man alienate people who might help him at a later date. My style, ingrained in my nature, has been to get people on my team by showing them I'm on theirs. Anyway, Fred, when he was at ABC, and I were in a pitched battle about when to put on the twenty-fifth anniversary show honoring the Bandstand. I wanted it on in prime time on a Saturday. Because he didn't think the show would have mass appeal, he suggested that we run it at a late hour—like eleven-thirty, after the news. In that time slot, I was sure that we would bomb. Fred, the boss in this matter, held his ground firmly—that is, until I figured out how to appeal to his nature.

"Here are two hundred fifty names," I said, thrusting into his hand a list of the greatest names in the entertainment business. "Pick out any eighty; I'll deliver them to the anniversary show—*if it's run in prime time.*"

He picked; the show ran in prime time (in fact, he expanded it to two hours) and it was a smash. I knew that Fred couldn't resist that kind of deal—especially when *he* would have the opportunity to select who would appear. I don't know how big Fred's ego is. Only his intimate friends could tell you that. As for mine, when the choice is between success—making something work—and my ego, winning always comes first. My ego knows how to fasten its seat belt and ride out a storm. I want to survive and thrive. Ego considerations come last.

We landed without a hitch at J.F.K.—the fates had respected my wishes. Or, perhaps, the gods had done a quick survey to see who would be willing to take over my workload and drew a blank. On an average day, I work on up to a dozen projects at one time, make a minimum of two hundred phone calls, and supervise a staff that sometimes runs in the hundreds. The private side of Dick Clark consists of more than the two T.V. shows on which I appear. I have a much greater involvement currently in my backstage business: running a highly successful production company that has made such winners as the Elvis Presley movie which ran on T.V. and is now showing in the theaters; and the Beatles movie which is just beginning its run. My survival instincts years ago told me that performing might not be a lasting career, and so I launched into the field of movie production and have prospered. Luckily, or otherwise, there seems to be no letup in my performing career. And so, I split my time between very full responsibilities. Yet, I feel young and, God knows, the world tells me I look young, too. The secret to my longevity is in the way I deal with my life, the successes, and, maybe even more, the failures.

As the taxi pulled away from the airport, I decided to utilize the half-hour trip to Manhattan as a rest period. I had a taping of a show to do that day and needed to be refreshed after the trying flight from the Coast. I dozed off and was nudged back into consciousness a while later by the driver as we arrived at the studio in midtown Manhattan.

The day went well. I still had a surplus of energy left, despite the trip, the taping, and the fifty phone calls I had made during breaks in the show. I came home to an empty apartment in the early evening and began to think about my ups and downs over all these years. Perhaps the flight had shaken me up more than I had realized because I seemed to be preoccupied with the issue of survival.

I remembered back to when I was a kid growing up in Mount Vernon. It was wartime. My brother, an idol for me as long as I could remember, was overseas. His absence had left a severe void in my life. I had always wanted to be like him: supremely confident, a star athlete, tall, and handsome. . . . When God gave out natural endowments, Brad was at the head of the list. By contrast, I was a skinny, short, pimply kid. I basked in the glory of Brad's successes. He, in turn, welcomed me into many of his activities. After he left to go overseas, I felt completely alone for the first time in my life. My parents were busy with their lives and with their worries about their fighter-pilot son. I turned to my schoolwork and also tried to emulate Brad.

I went out for contact sports, despite my small size. I tried, without much success, to come off confident with friends and, especially, with girls. There was no way that a pimply little guy like me was going to be able to measure up to Brad—his shoes were just too big to fill.

Coming home from school one day, I paused to pick up the newspaper in the lobby of our apartment building and was confronted by our friendly building superintendent.

"I'm really sorry," Mr. Lindblum said. "I know just how you felt about Brad."

I held the newspaper up to my face, pretending to read the comics. Inside, my heart pounded. I knew, but didn't want to know, what Mr. Lindblum had meant. Death wasn't possible, not for Brad. In fact, the word "dead" was only a word. "Dying" was an abstraction, not a reality. What did it mean? I didn't want to know the answer.

Upstairs, my parents were steeped in a grief too large for me to comprehend. Mother was destroyed. I had never seen her that way. She never recovered from that loss. My father, usually an emotionally reserved person, wept. His sobs penetrated to the core. I cried for hours.

In the ensuing days, my emotions took various paths: from anger that Brad was taken away from me, to diffuse blame at those who could have let that happen, to pride that my brother died a war hero on a fighter-pilot mission in the Battle of the Bulge. I was determined, more than ever, to be just like him and, in a way, to live out his unfinished life.

I redoubled my efforts to be a sports star. I almost perished in the attempt! Getting your face stepped on can humble anyone—especially a five-foot-nine high school football player like me. I couldn't make my body do what Brad's had been able to do. My confident walk (modeled after Brad's) was not the same as his was, naturally. He was a born winner, and I (I began to believe) was destined to be a loser. Then I had the kind of insight that comes out of frustration and failure: I could never win playing by my brother's rules. That single thought, more than any other, sprung loose my hidden potential.

As it became clear that I was *me*, not a scaled-down version of my brother, several things happened: firstly, my sadness at his passing intensified temporarily. I had to learn to say good-bye to Brad for good, including his unfinished business here on earth. He was gone, and so, too, was the hope that a Clark son would be a tall, athletic hero. His desire to win would have to be matched by my own as a tribute to him, but in a domain where I could succeed. The second result of my realization that Brad, and the goals his life represented, were gone for good was that I had a clean slate to work with. I could set a course for myself and win using my own rules. I felt relieved, in a way, that my life was now at square one. I knew that I would have to find my own way and began to sense an inner conviction that I could do just that. Brad's passing taught me just how fragile life really was and how important it was for me to take charge right now! The sudden removal of his protection and his example as a trailblazer led to a rude but important awakening in me: I was now *it*. It would be do or die for me, alone, from now on. I was determined to make it.

As Churchill once said, after the Allies had beaten the Germans badly in Africa, "It wasn't the beginning of the end. It was the end of the beginning." Brad's death had made me mature quickly and take stock of my life. I saw no future for myself in athletics. Lucky for me I realized that. Somehow, I don't think I could have added anything to the

world of professional football . . . except as a peanut ven-dor.

I asked myself: "What do I do best—what do I like to do just for fun?" The answer was obvious. I had always loved the performing arts. Any aspect of the entertainment busi-ness had always been able to capture my fascinated atten-tion. I set out to chart my own future as a performer. It became easier to live the rest of my high school and college years after I had made up my mind to build a life around who I really was rather than to base one after Brad's image.

Years later, as I surveyed my career with all the succes-ses I have had, I realize that this one event—Brad's death and its results—was central to my achievements. I know who I am and what I can and cannot do. I play my hand from strength at all times.

In my lifetime, I have had to take many big gambles—risks of several million dollars on one deal are com-monplace in the movie production business. I must know, in each case, that the bet is a safe one. The only way I can be sure of that is to bet on my strengths—and to do that, I must be totally candid with myself, not trying to pretend I am anything other than what I really am. To let ego get in the way of business judgment is fatal. I know how to play my hand because I don't bullshit myself about the cards I hold. If you don't read any farther than this, you have already gotten the essence of my story.

I apply this principle of honesty to other people, as well. As a producer, I have to bet on other people's talents in order to win. I can't afford the luxury of diplomacy when it is suggested that I bet millions on a questionable talent. I have to know what someone can offer, what kind of con-tribution they can make to a show or movie, and work from there. Too much money can be lost by trying to be Mr. Nice Guy and allowing sentiment to cloud business decisions. There are people in the entertainment business whom I love dearly; but I would not have them work for me because they don't recognize their own limitations and want me to back their blindness with my hard cash and reputation. I know I must sound like a son-of-a-bitch, not like the Dick Clark you saw on "American Bandstand" whose only duty was to keep up the pace of the show for sixty fun-filled minutes. But, in business and in life, you must not allow other people's weakness to become the basis for your actions, no matter how much you like them.

On the other hand, I have made a fortune by identifying talent in people who were unaware of what they had to offer. I remember one such situation: I was putting together a show to play in Vegas. I needed a comedian, and the name of an old friend came to mind. He'd been through many legal difficulties and was blackballed in the business. It had been years since he'd worked. His confidence was depleted.

I told my staff that I would be using him as my comedy act. The response was a thunderous, "You're suicidal! Don't you know what this guy has done to his reputation—what he can do to yours?"

I replied, "I also know what he's capable of doing to an audience if he's on. I'll see that he feels confident about me at first. Maybe, if he can borrow my confidence for a while, he'll work out."

When I approached the individual in question, he refused. "I can't do that to you, Dick. We're old friends. You'll be tarnished by your association with me. Thanks, but no, thanks."

I wouldn't take no for an answer. I pressed him with all I had until he accepted. He was a smash. His career rocketed back to the top. I made a fortune on the tour with him as a top-billed act. He's never forgotten my confidence in him and has repaid my favor manifold. Betting on human nature is an excellent risk, provided you clear the sentimentality and self-delusion out of your judgment.

My mind was tiring. The frightening plane trip, the taping, all the phone calls, and the solitary late-night philosophizing had finally drained my energy. I fell asleep peacefully, having survived another hectic, successful day.

I awoke the next morning with my battery fully charged. It was going to be a big day for my production company. We were getting ready to do the Beatles movie. There was a person whom I was anxious to sign for a starring role. I was going to meet with him to discuss terms when his agent called.

"Dick, it doesn't look good. My client would like to do the movie, but he has a prior commitment to do another film that overlaps yours. I'm worried that he'll get caught in a conflict and have to bow out at the last minute. Since the other deal was made first, we'd have to leave you in the lurch. That we'd never do. Sorry, old buddy, but we'll have to pass on this one."

"What if I can clear things with the other producer? Will he do the movie if I can change their production schedule?"

"They'll never do it. You know how that studio is about things like that."

"Can I try?" I begged.

"Go ahead, if it'll make you sleep better."

In my enthusiasm, I almost hung up on him before saying, "Thanks a million."

In trying to sort out this mess, I ran into a hornet's nest of problems. Actor's Equity in England threatened to strike if I used an American actor in a lead role. In turn, I threatened to pull the whole production out of that country. The union decided that it was better to play ball with us than to lose the work for their members. They decided to pull back their demand. Then the problem of making arrangements to obtain the services of the actor I wanted who had made a prior commitment came up. I decided to go right into the eye of the hurricane.

I called the other producer who had him under contract and laid out the problem, straight. "I can't change my production schedule for the following reasons," I said, enumerating the jam-ups I was facing on this project. "I know you have more room to play with in your movie. If you give way this time, I'll owe you a big one."

The other producer agreed to move his schedule around to suit our shooting timetable. I owe him a big favor. He knows I'll come through. The lesson of this episode is: "bulldog determination is a key survival asset."

I never accept, at face value, that anything is impossible. After all, problems are made by people and can be solved by them. In this case, the conflict in schedules was a starting point for my efforts to get the actor, not an end point, as it would have been for so many people. I take each problem and break it down into steps:

- Who are the key decision-makers in this issue?
- What do they stand to lose if they decide in my favor?
- If they help me out, what will they get in return— what's their payoff for playing ball with me?

I try to weight pro's and con's of the other guy's moves, knowing that, only if it is good for the other side will the deal have a chance. Have you ever been able to sell someone on an idea until they could see the benefits? This lesson about business negotiations I learned way back in my college days as a Fuller Brush salesman.

In those days, I needed the cash badly and so I took the

best job I could get—and that was door-to-door selling. The earliest lesson I learned in that vocation was that people want to buy; you don't have to create that motivation in them. What you *must* do is to give a person a good reason to be nice to himself or herself. So, if the hairbrush won't sell because the woman thinks it would be too self-indulgent to spend five dollars on a new bristle hairbrush, take out the toilet bowl brush. Maybe she'll feel less guilty about buying a work tool than a luxury item. One way or another, you sell her something—you must never take "No" for an answer.

In the world of business, you also must never say die. There is always some strategy that will work. If it's not this formula, then some other combination will click. The magic is in your own undying efforts to find the right solution. As sure as you and I are alive, there is some workable solution—you need only search for it long and hard enough. It will be there, staring you in the face at some point.

Having broken through the greatest obstacles to the success of the Beatles movie, I handed the project back to one of my assistants and went to the studio to tape another T.V. show. Audiences turn me on; I will always be a performer in fact or at heart.

There was ample time before the taping began for me to nip back to my apartment and change clothes in the comfort of home rather than in a tiny dressing room. As I walked the few blocks to my apartment, my thoughts drifted back to my beginnings in show business.

I was a kid, just turned twenty, and needed work. I wanted to break into broadcasting and applied for a position at a station in Utica. I was put off for a month and then finally was given a chance to go on the air. I did extremely well. The station was small, but it was a perfect place for me to learn and develop confidence. I plowed a tremendous amount of effort into my work, questioning the old pros on their trade secrets and taking in everything that I heard or saw. The jobs came fast and furious after that first one. Since that time, I have never been out of work in my life. It would have been very easy for me to get into a rut and stay there. After all, I had wanted to work in broadcasting, and, early on, I had reached my goal. Why change courses so many times as I have done?

I remember, in those years, my constant dream: to get into the biggest market I could find, on the best show I could land. Maybe, I still wanted to live out my brother's heroic destiny. I was always willing to pull up roots and make a move to a bigger challenge and a higher level of exposure. When the time came to take a shot at the big time, I cried when I left home to go to Philadelphia. Those tears kept flowing all the way up the New York State Thruway, and down the Turnpike until I reached Philly. I was taking a step down, from my own T.V. show in Utica to a radio announcer's job in Philadelphia on WFIL. The lure of the big time was irresistible. I had to go to a bigger city if I was ever to really make it. I knew my destiny was in the direction away from security. I left home and wept my way to Philadelphia, and to fame and fortune.

My nostalgic reminiscing was interrupted by my arrival at my apartment building. The phone was ringing as I entered the apartment. It was Kari, the woman I love and am married to. Her voice is the greatest high for me, especially when I'm away from home and working like a beaver.

"Happy birthday, Dick. How are you, love?"

"Fine. I miss you. I'll be home tomorrow. Sorry we couldn't celebrate together. Keep my birthday cake in the refrigerator. And skip the candles! They're getting to be an embarrassment."

"Dick, I'm afraid I have bad news. They're cancelling the variety show," Kari said softly.

Kari's news hit me like a thunderbolt. I had planned and prepared all my life to do an Ed Sullivan type of variety show. When Fred Silverman was at ABC (my network at that time), we disagreed on the merits of the project. I had told my good friends at the network that I was planning to shop around to sell the variety show idea.

NBC bought it. Soon after that, they also hired Fred Silverman as president. I knew the show was doomed from that moment on. But, anticipating death isn't ever adequate preparation for its impact. I was stunned, saddened. Mr. Lindblum's face flashed in front of my eyes. I couldn't hide behind a newspaper to escape reality as I had done when he announced my brother's death. I felt as did Adlai Stevenson upon losing the election to Ike: "like a boy who had stubbed his toe: I was too old to cry, yet it hurt too much to ignore." I took stock while Kari waited for my response at the other end of the line.

"I've got twenty great things just waiting to take off. We'll survive," I said.

"I know we will, love," she replied, her voice quivering with compassion.

2

Setting Out on Your Journey to Success

"I'm sure you've seen the bumper stickers that read: I BRAKE FOR ANIMALS. If someone ever put a slogan on a bumper sticker that epitomized my philosophy, it would be: I DON'T BRAKE FOR DISASTERS. Long ago, when my brother died, I learned that work was the best antidote for depression. Reminding myself that, despite my grief, I was alive and had to keep going was what pulled me through. My mother, who stopped in her tracks as a result of that loss, never fully recovered.

Since that experience, I have dealt with disappointment by renewing my forward movement with increased vigor. When I was divorced and my ex-wife was awarded an extremely large settlement, I set out with single-minded determination to make good that financial loss. Within two years I had recouped all the money I had paid out to her. When I lost the variety show, I was stunned, but only momentarily. I don't believe in wallowing in grief. My approach to a loss is to learn from it so I won't have to repeat the same sad experience if it is at all preventable.

If you find yourself ruminating after a loss or disappointment, ask yourself:

- Am I wallowing?
- Or, are my thoughts about this defeat an effort to learn how to avoid similar ones in the future?

If you detect that you are wallowing, cut loose that type of wasteful thinking. You can benefit even from defeat, if you dig in and find your Achilles' heel. Then, put the whole lesson in your memory and continue your forward movement. Wallowing feeds on itself and tends to go on forever. Learning from defeat is a self-limited operation: once a lesson is learned, your mind clears up and you can go forward with renewed enthusiasm. But there is a critical requirement here that will guarantee your survival: you must have a direction in life!

When you know the route you are traveling, a temporary detour into defeat will only delay you for a short time. But what happens if you have no sense of your own destiny? You are thrown off track and feel like all is lost. You try to recover but don't know what you must do, where you must go to accomplish that rescue operation.

When I lost the variety show that I had worked toward for twenty-five years of my life, I still hadn't lost my direction. I was sustained by the knowledge that I had a clear path charted toward success. I was reassured by my ability to have come as far as I had already come. What remained was to set out once more on my journey to success, without delay! You won't find me hanging around the burned-out shell of my defeats too long. There are too many good opportunities waiting for me out there.

I try to pass on this philosophy to people I encounter. Since travel is such a large part of my life, I meet lots of people in airports. Being a celebrity, I am noticed and the braver souls strike up conversations with me. One such experience occurred some time ago at J.F.K. Airport.

My flight to California was delayed. I was sitting in the lounge, deep in thought about future projects. My mind raced back and forth from the politics of the entertainment industry—something I have quite a good grip on—to my several nemeses in this business. Suddenly, my consciousness was diverted to a figure who towered over me, dressed in a khaki uniform.

"You're Dick Clark," said the soldier.

"Yes. What's your name?" I asked, and then felt foolish as I noticed the name plate on his uniform.

"Briggs, sir . . . Tommy Briggs," he replied with military respect.

"Where are you from, Tom?"

"Scranton, sir," he replied stiffly.

Motioning to the empty seat beside me, I said, "Sit down, Tom."

He accepted my invitation nervously.

"I guess we're on the same flight, Mr. Clark. Do you live in California?" he asked, trying to fill a void in our conversation that was a moment to me and an eternity to him.

"Yes, I live in L.A. and also have a place in New York. Where are you going, Tom?"

"I'm going back to my base to be discharged. Then I'm going to head back to Scranton."

"You have a career lined up back home?" I inquired.

"No. . . . Going back to Scranton is just the natural thing to do, I guess. That's where I grew up."

"What do you dream about as far as a career is concerned?" I probed.

Tom's eyes lit up. "I really want to get into some business of my own. But I don't have that kind of dough just now," he said, his enthusiastic tone beginning to wilt.

"Where would you like to set up your business, whenever that day comes?" I pursued.

"On the West Coast. I love California and want to settle down there someday." His voice regained some eagerness.

"So why the heck go back to Scranton?" I asked rhetorically. "Your destiny is in a business on the West Coast. The government owes you an education and a ticket to wherever you call home. Why not stay out West after you're discharged and start down the road to your dream right now?"

"You make it sound so easy," he said, smiling.

"It's just as easy or easier to chart a course and follow it as to grind it out each day with no direction," I replied.

"I guess so," he agreed, some mild hesitation in his voice.

"Here's my card, Tom," I said, pressing my business card into his hand. "I want to hear from you after you leave the service. Let me know how your dream is coming along, okay?"

"You bet," he replied, his eyes sparkling with delight.

I haven't yet heard from Tom, but I hope he took my advice to heart. Charting a direction for your life is more important than anything else, if you want to be a survivor in this world. While others wander about aimlessly, expending energy on a quest which has no stable reference points, you will always have your bearings. When you are thrown off track, your dream will be the navigational beacon to guide you back on course.

My flight to L.A. brought me into the midst of a beehive of activity. My staff had been busily working for some time to fulfill our end of the biggest deal in T.V. history.

Some days earlier, a little envelope imprinted with the NBC logo had arrived conveying an offer of $20,000,000 for the services of my related production companies over the coming three years. It was a "pay or play" contract, meaning that I would produce shows for the network and would be paid for them, whether or not they were used. Numerous people had to be hired. My existing staff had been too small to handle the volume of production called for in the contract. I had to secure the rights to excellent properties to put on television. My mind had toiled while my staff celebrated. Wild enthusiasm is the luxury of the follower, not the leader. For me, there was no losing sight of my direction, even though that contract brought my dream closer than ever before.

My day was used up before I realized. I started for home and a well-deserved rest. During my trip home, earlier victories came to mind.

Years ago, when I was offered the spot on "American Bandstand," I recall how frightened I was. The previous host had been fired after being charged with statutory rape. The show needed a great deal of image rebuilding. I was going to be the person who would make everyone forget the scandal-ridden headlines. Luckily for me, the offer to replace the previous host was made long before Watergate. Had Watergate come first, I'm sure I would have concluded that I'd end up just like Gerald Ford, the guy who attempted to clean up that mess and got turned out of office for his efforts. In any case, I was scared but willing, so I accepted the job. I had worked too hard to position myself for success to turn away now. That opportunity was the reason I had left the comfort and security of home and had come to a big city, Philadelphia. I realized that, to get into the big time, I had to get closer to the action. Now, I was being handed this somewhat tarnished piece of jewelry, and it was my duty to polish it back to its original luster. I accepted the job.

The first lesson I learned from this is that when you see the "big chance" come your way, seize it with all its imperfections. Sure the show had a serious reputation problem to overcome. If that problem hadn't existed, I'd never have been given the chance to host. Any time a great opportunity exists, there is always a little mud caked on it. Nobody gives away blue-white diamonds. But you will be frequently offered rocks that can be cut and polished into gems. The moral of the story of my early beginnings on the "Bandstand" is that all great deals have imperfections. If you want to succeed, you have to accept that it is your responsibility to clean up the mess that preceded you—you must set right the screw-up that frightened everyone else away and left the field open for your big chance!

I had set my sights on the big time, and at a tender age, in my early twenties, there I was . . . success was at hand. The Hollywood script would now show me rising to the top in meteoric fashion. They'd have me pictured riding down Main Street of my old hometown in a Cadillac, with throngs lining the street throwing confetti or ticker tape at me to celebrate a hometown boy having made it in the big time. The real story is far different.

Instead of a Cadillac and a ticker tape parade, would you believe an old chartered bus riding down a deserted highway at 2 A.M.? I knew that, to make it, I would have to be a promoter. And promote I did! I toured endlessly with musical groups to stir up interest in Rock and Roll. I insisted on eating and sleeping with the troops, even though I was earning a great deal of money by the standards of those days and could easily have afforded to fly first class and stay in the best hotels. However, I wanted to inspire the confidence of performer and fan alike. To do this, I had to be credible to the people who made the show a success. I wanted to be with my performers and fans, not above them. Hence, the long, dreary bus rides from town to town.

My experience selling Fuller Brush products in college came into play. I went out and sold the T.V. show to agencies. I kept on selling until the show was completely and solidly booked. You'd think that I could let up at that point, wouldn't you? Not so.

I realized that my destiny was in the hands of network executives. Somehow, I have less than average faith in some of their judgment. My recent experience only justifies my low opinion of some of these transients who, during their brief stay in office, try to axe as many careers as they can as a tribute to their virility. In any case, I was not going to let my success or failure in show business be decided by a half-asleep executive who looked in the mirror one morning while shaving and decided that "Dick Clark just has to go."

I decided to get a wall of protection built around my show. The key people in the television industry are station managers. They are the ones who recognize which shows are making profits for them. I got to know each and every manager at all the stations that carried the show. I tried to remember their spouse's name, their birthday, and anything else that was important to their lives. I wanted them on my team. I wanted them to keep me on their team. To this day, after twenty-seven years running a sold-out show, I still call station managers to see how the "Bandstand" is doing for them and to wish them Merry Christmas.

Don't let anyone sell you on the Hollywood version of lasting fame and fortune. Sure, it's possible to get a lucky break and, as Andy Warhol has said, "to be famous for fifteen minutes." Anyone can get to the summit. I am convinced of that fact. But staying there—surviving there—requires a totally different strategy.

To be a survivor, you must know how to position yourself for success. You can only do that if you have a road map and know where you are headed. Maintaining your dream, despite all disappointments, provides you with the road map to success.

Next, you must be capable of recognizing that your big chance will often appear less than ideal when you first see it. It will be clouded or flawed. That's why it was there, lying around, unnoticed, just waiting for you to take it.

You must be a promoter to get that dream to the stage of reality. And then, when success has been achieved, you must realize that it is only a starting point. You will be required to defend your dream against all attacks so that it will endure. Survivors never cease to be vigilant. Longevity in any business is won by laying out a survival plan for the near and distant future. That's why, when my $20,000,000 contract arrived at my offices, my staff drank champagne while I plotted and planned how to sustain the forward momentum.

Each quantum leap in your career is stressful as hell. From being secretary, you are promoted to administrative assistant. The pay and status are higher. But so is the level of stress. Now, you are expected to be your boss's eyes, ears, and memory. You must step out from behind the boss's shadow and be recognized as a person in your own right. No longer can you afford to say, "I'll take it up with Mr. Jones." You are expected to make decisions and take responsibility. Most people feel inadequate when first confronted with a major new challenge. I'm no exception.

I have a little show business remedy for this type of stress. Fake it!

Whenever I have to deal with a major challenge—something brand-new for which my previous experience has not been a sufficient preparation—I think to myself, "Nobody is born with the skill to do this job. If I appear to be uncertain, those around me will inspect my work with a magnifying glass at best, or will hover around me like vultures, waiting for my ultimate demise to see how they can benefit from it, at worst." Either prospect would only increase my stress and undermine my already shaky skills. So I fake confidence. I act *as if* I really have the situation under control. People then go about their business as usual while I hurry up and learn how the hell to do the job.

In almost everything—from sex, to parenthood, to work—you first must *do*; then you learn what you're doing. At every level of my career, I've started out looking great on the outside, but shaking in my boots inside. Since my ego never prevents me from asking stupid questions, I quickly learn to master a situation with an air of composure. Stupid questions asked with confidence appear to be "deeper than what meets the eye."

"He can't be asking that dumb question," reasons the sage. "He appears so confident. There must be a deeper meaning to his query that goes beyond my ability to comprehend." The sage, feeling thoroughly intimidated by now, answers my question at face value, convinced he must have missed the entire thrust of my inquiry. I calmly accept his explanation and gain an answer while covering my tracks. Act as if you know what you're doing and the smokescreen will last long enough to cover your inadequacy until you really know what the hell is going on. If your ignorance is discovered, your aplomb will deter any ridicule. Once you are confident of your ego, it won't let you down. It is totally impossible for me to feel like a fool even when I'm asking foolish questions.

Driving home from my California office, feeling exhausted but gratified, I asked myself, "Do big money deals make *me*, or do I make these deals? Is my confidence a product of fame and fortune; or is success something a person has within, that eventually links up with the right opportunity?"

I'm not a believer in destiny from an astrological or even a genetic standpoint. I'm convinced that winners are self-created. Some people, with no greater talent or brains than anyone else, set out for the stars and reach their goal. Others get lost or discouraged along the way and fail.

As I drove home on the Freeway, my mind played back and forth between my most recent achievement and the earlier origins of my success. I became more and more convinced that by taking stock of my strengths and planning carefully, I could be a winner in any field I chose. I happened to select show business. But the ingredients for my success in that field could help me make it to the top in any pursuit.

The world's best milkman would be so confident of himself that he would act with authority in any situation and, hence, would easily master a wide variety of skills outside milk delivery. This broadening-out of abilities is something that is necessary for lasting success. Once you're an ace in one arena, you're given respect in all others. And, if you're smart, you translate that acknowledgment into fame and fortune.

"Tonight, on our show, we have a real treat for you," says Johnny Carson. "Bill Button, the world's greatest milkman, is with us to discuss his new best-selling book, *Why Not the Breast?*"

If you're King of Milkmen, you'll soon figure out a way to make it in books, show business, real estate, or in any field you so desire. I was the King of Dance Show Hosts. From that start, I made it to being a successful movie producer, a collector of rare cars, and an investor in a wide variety of businesses such as a broadcasting company and the Westchester Premier Theater. Longevity in my business or yours starts from being a winner in one area and spreading out laterally. You can't afford to perch your success upon a narrow base in one field. As soon as you can, do like Bill Button, King of Milkmen: translate your mastery in one endeavor into opportunities in many others. The success formula in one field can easily be applied in any other. I'm not the first person to recognize that fact.

A top executive in a bicycle manufacturing company could succeed as president of a company that produces linguine. Winners are winners, no matter where they are. The key strategy for long-term survival is to try to achieve success in as many aspects of your field as you can, and, if possible, to diversify into as many other fields as you can handle. Confidence is contagious. Winning is a habit you get into. Don't stop once you have gotten the knack of it.

As I headed down the Freeway, I came upon a traffic jam of monumental proportions. I thought: "Even a big-dollar contract won't make this traffic move any faster." I bolted off the Freeway at an exit and explored alternate routes home, using local streets. The thought came to mind that, in an interesting way, finding detours was a vital ingredient of success in my career. Whenever I saw a block to my forward progress, rather than curse my fate, I hastened to find a way around the obstruction. It's one thing to have a well-laid-out road map to success. It's another thing to follow it slavishly, even though the roads that appear clear in your plans turn out to be blocked in reality.

Finding a detour around obstructions has been as frequent a task for me as driving straight up the road to success. If you get stuck in traffic jams, your career may never reach its full potential, and, certainly, you will tire of the endless delays and settle for less than you set out to achieve.

In setting out on a journey to success, you can't ever conceive of how far and wide your ultimate achievements will range. Hence, it is necessary to set initial goals. Then, when they are reached or approached, set new goals that are more ambitious and far-reaching.

I must be a workaholic, but, if so, I'm one of the most contented ones in the world. I always set artifically high goals. If I can do five jobs in one day, I soon move it to six. If six can be done, why not seven . . . eight . . . then nine? My energy is not depleted by hard work. Like a well-trained athlete, work invigorates me. Challenges feed me energy which I use to reach loftier goals. Eventually I reach an outer limit where I know I must stop and rest . . . for now!

My detour had brought me home with little time lost. I went to my room, changed, dove into the ocean, and began to think: "How the hell an I going to produce $20,000,000 worth of quality television? And how will I pyramid this deal to something even bigger?"

3

Taking Charge

What goes through your mind when you think of taking charge of your life? Do you see yourself in a master control room with a myriad of switches and dials with multicolored flashing lights, artfully manipulating this electronic control panel? Or do you see a crowd of people gathering around to pay homage to your mastery over life? Perhaps your fantasies are simpler. Maybe your idea of being in charge of your life is simply knowing that the bills are being paid on time and that the most important relationships are coming along okay.

Many people feel that taking charge is an overwhelming task—something for the ilk of a General George Patton, Gloria Steinem, or John F. Kennedy. They believe that life is too complex and changeable to ever get a handle on it. Instead, they settle for becoming passively responsive to crisis—taking charge only when forced to by circumstances, or learning to adjust to adversity—but never seeking out opportunities for mastery in advance.

My life has taught me that taking charge requires neither the backbone of a General Patton, the intellect of a Gloria Steinem, nor the charisma of a John F. Kennedy. All that is necessary is a simple understanding of what is entailed in the process of taking charge. The key word is DETAIL.

Do you ever notice the I.B.M. ads? They emphasize the value of their computers through pointing out how these machines give you control over information. If I remember correctly, the copy reads: "We put you in touch with *reality*." Their pitch to a business executive who is struggling to take charge of his or her operation equates information management with being in touch with reality. I couldn't agree more!

Keeping your finger on the pulse of things means being on top of detail all the time! Only that way can you know what is really happening in your life and begin to master it. In business, computers help you track detail, thus keeping you one step *ahead* of crisis. In life, since you have no handy little computer to help you out, you must rely on your brain to keep on top of things. Come to think of it, your brain *is* a computer. It's a more sophisticated computer than any ever invented, past or present. In my estimation, your brain is the best computer that will ever exist on the face of the earth—provided you know how to work it!

Clearly, I am no scientist or psychologist. So don't expect a technical discourse here on how the cerebral cortex works on a cellular level. However, you and I can be expert at using our brains as computers without knowing the intricacies of the neurological wiring. I have an exotic car and am a damned good driver, yet I don't know one thing about how to pull apart the fuel-injection system to repair it. You don't have to know the wiring diagram of a computer to be able to use its terminal to keep on top of things.

Your brain and mine are amazingly easy to use. Just let

the darned thing do its job—don't confuse it with pessimism or optimism—and it will keep track of the most complex situations, always coming up with useful answers and insights. Your biological memory bank is infinite relative to your day-to-day needs. Yet, as we all know, most of us use only a fraction of the brain's capacity at any time.

Here's how I try to maximize the abilities of my brain in taking charge of a situation:

1. I never rush things. My brain can only work as fast as it was designed to. I never try to get an answer faster than the next person. I just try to arrive at the right answer.

2. I listen to everyone, even to my opponents. The brain works best when it is given the most information possible with which to operate. Now, don't get me wrong here. Many people, myself included, feel more comfortable with black-and-white issues. "Don't confuse me with the facts, please," is a dangerous, yet enticing, frame of mind.

   I make it a point to ask advice of my adversaries as well as my friends. You'd be amazed how disarming it is when you ask an opponent, "What would you do if you were on my side of the negotiation at this point?" The usual response is an offer of your adversary's opinion, which, in most cases, is sincere and helpful. All information, including that coming from opponents, is valuable in getting a situation under control.

3. I never lose sight of the bottom line. When entering into a negotiation or a new situation, my first request is, "Tell me the core of the problem. I'll get to the plumbing later on." Why waste time on a complex deal if the payoff is small or wrong for me? First, I try

to isolate the essence of the problem. Then I work out the minute details.

4. I keep track of all aspects of a situation, no matter how many experts are working along with me. Ultimately, I'm responsible for my successes or failures. Hence, I want to know, at every moment, that everything possible is being done to bring a situation to a successful conclusion. I have the strongest vested interest in all my enterprises, and so I must put the most into ensuring their success.

5. I know when not to make a decision. I never decide anything when I'm tired or moody. I don't want to be swayed by my own optimism or pessimism, and so I make every decision many times before coming to any final conclusions.

I deliberate about a big decision on a relaxed afternoon at the beach. That brings my creative mind to bear on the problem. Then, having formed an opinion, I come at the problem all over again in my office, where my hard-nosed business mind has a crack at the issue. Before going ahead, I discuss the situation with my wife, Kari, to get her input. She usually takes the human aspect of the situation more into account, focusing on the personalities involved in the deal—whether or not the chemistry will work. Only by making the decision in many different contexts can I come up with consistently correct answers. Come to think of it, that's the way an I.B.M. computer works, isn't it? The computer makes multiple correlations, comparing all the data in different combinations with all the other data until it comes up with the right answer. See, I told you your brain is a damned good computer!

It's one thing to know how to use your brain, and another thing to use it. Many people fail to act in situations that require decisiveness, even though, if you asked them, they would know exactly what to do and how to do it. Why?

Most people operate on the basis of their weaknesses rather than their strengths. They plan their lives around fears, not abilities.

- "I can't do it. I'll look like a fool if I fail."
- "There's too much at stake. I won't be able to live with a failure of this magnitude."
- "I'll try it next time, after someone else shows the way."

The litany of losers is replete with such phrases. They begin to believe their own words and hold back, even in situations where they could take charge and win.

My philosophy is the extreme opposite.

- "I'll try to do it. I don't give a damn if I look like a fool. Chances are I'll succeed and look like a hero. And if I fail, so what? I'll keep trying until I win."
- "There's a lot at stake. Great! That'll keep the losers away and leave the field open for me."
- "I'll try it first, before everyone realizes how easy it is. I'll get the jump on everyone. My head start is their fear versus my confidence."

In business and in life, you must base your actions on an expectation of winning. Make all your plans as a believer and you will prevail. But if you are your own worst detractor, your greatest fears will be realized. Your paralysis will be your greatest stumbling block. Confidence and attention to detail have been my greatest assets over the years, both in business and in my personal life.

One of the nicest things I am ever asked to do is help out at a ceremony honoring a friend. I recently was involved in one such situation which points out almost everything I have described about taking charge in a situation.

The scene is a fancy dinner to honor a man who engineered one of the most successful charity fund-raising efforts in history. The audience, three times as many people as were expected to attend, is restless in their formal attire as speaker after speaker drones on. To add to their misery, the sound system is so poor that you can hardly hear what is being said from the podium. The entire event threatens to be a shambles—a humiliation of a man who deserves high praise, instead. Nobody in the audience moves a muscle. Despite the fact that in the audience are assembled the best brains of the broadcast industry, not one soul gets up to see what can be done to improve the sound system.

Finally, I leave my seat at the head table and head backstage. The sound man is off in a corner, one hand deep in his pocket, the other hand holding a girlie magazine. He is startled when he sees me standing over him.

"I will personally castrate you if that sound system isn't working right in ten seconds!" I bark at him, with every intention of making good my threat.

"Yes, sir," he says fearfully, running off to his sound console.

As I re-enter the hall, the keynote speaker is on the podium, beginning to give the most awful speech I have ever heard.

She's a politician, speaking to a group of Jewish business people at a time when her ties to the administration remind everyone in the audience of the arm-twisting her boss is doing to the Israeli Prime Minister. Instead of being tactful and humorous, she launches into an attempt at being profound. Disasters usually come in clusters. I get to the podium and decide to take charge.

Knowing that she has lost the audience entirely, I decide to tell a white lie.

"Ladies and gentlemen," I begin. "I feel a bit embarrassed for the last speaker because I know how bad the sound system has been and that many of you were unable to hear all her remarks." I decide to blame the problem on the P.A. system rather than on her lousy speech. I go on: "The reason for our problem tonight is that three times the expected number showed up to honor our esteemed colleague. Sometimes, paying tribute to a great man has its price, too." I continue with remarks directed to the guest of honor's achievements, the bottom line for why everyone showed up. The evening gets back on track.

The possession of exceptional faculties for solving problems is only as valuable as the use to which they are put. With a room full of people from the entertainment field, in both the performing and technical areas, not one person moved to save the evening. That's why so many people don't get to the top, even though they have what it takes. That's why so many people don't stay at the top, even though they get there at one time.

I'm a successful producer because I put all my abilities to work *all the time!* Not because I'm brighter than all the rest of the people in California and New York.

When I arrived back on the East Coast to begin working on my network T.V. deal, I had planned to visit an old friend with whom I had started out years back in the early days of the "Bandstand." I had wanted first to stop off at the studio in New York, tape a few segments of the "Pyramid," and then head off to Philadelphia to visit Phil, who I heard was sick. My assistant at the studio called me aside as soon as I arrived and said, "Phil's wife called. She said he's dying. Come as soon as you can."

Those words went through me like a knife. Phil was a beloved friend who grew up with me in the business. Even though he once disappointed me in the worst way, I forgave him and continued to love him dearly. The knowledge of his illness had saddened me, but I never expected the end to come this soon. I asked my assistant to order a limousine to drive me to Philadelphia right away, and I left the studio.

The late-night trip was filled with memories. I was traveling down the same road to Philadelphia I had driven down years earlier when leaving Utica to strike out for fame and fortune. I had cried the first time out of fear and loneliness. This time, I wept over the disappointments and joys of the past.

The payola hearings in Washington came to mind. I was facing the panel of congressmen and defending myself against accusations that were without foundation. Phil had done a few things, probably in innocence, and, given the political mood of the day, his actions came under close scrutiny. In the course of the hearings, I found he had let me down badly. I faced the investigation with all my homework done and was exonerated. Yet, Phil became associated in my mind with that extreme unpleasantness. Riding down a dark highway to his deathbed, I felt a surge of the pain I had felt when told, many years back, of his indiscretion. Somehow, when people die, we feel that they are letting us down, even though we know that they aren't doing this by choice. I wept on the way to the hospital, remembering all we had been through together—the joys and agonies—and realizing that a beloved friendship was about to end.

I arrived at his room to find utter confusion. The family was milling around in the waiting area. His tearful wife, drained of energy from keeping a vigil at this side, was unable to organize this sad scene. I stepped in and played traffic cop. Phil was comatose but alive. I knew it was important for the children to see him one last time. One by one, I led them to their father's side and put my arm around them as they held their father's hand for a last farewell. And then he died.

Taking charge is something you must do with tears running down your cheeks and a lump, the size of a grapefruit, in your throat.

The trip back to New York was a time for recovery and renewal. I was in the midst of plans to develop that year's American Music Awards show to compete with the Grammys. Way back, when I was asked whether I could do such a show, I had answered, "Yes," assuming that I would figure out a way to pull it off at a later date. Then came the job of bringing this dream to fruition.

I had wanted this show to be more than just a knock-off of the Grammy Awards. In the latter, the selections are made by several hundred people in the music industry. The thought had come to me: "Why not give everyone a chance to pick their favorites?" Although the idea seemed like a winner, I had to convince the executive who had assigned the show to me on the merits of conducting a broad-based public poll.

I remember dashing about my apartment furiously, gathering up record albums. Then I hurried over to the hotel where the network executive was staying.

"Here is the cast for the award show," I remember saying to him, laying out the albums on his bed. He had known me for twenty years and believed me when I said that I could deliver all these performers.

"How many people did you say you wanted to poll for the American Music Awards?" he asked with some skepticism.

"About thirty-five thousand," I replied coolly.

"I'll leave it up to you to make it work," he said in a mildly challenging tone.

I'll make it work," I replied. And make it work we did!

We had never before done an award show. I felt like a high school kid who had taken a dare. I wasn't going to back down for anything, whatever the cost. We recruited the very best people in the industry. Having many old friends for whom you have done favors in the past helps on such an occasion. We analyzed every other award show—the Grammys, the Emmys, the Oscars—and plugged all the holes. We developed a system, since copied by every other award show, to make certain that we had a power-packed start to the show with winner after winner. In the changeover period—the hourly and half-hourly station breaks—we made sure that nobody would switch to another channel by starting special entertainment packages at four minutes before the breaks and running them until four minutes after. We didn't lose one viewer. And those who flipped channels during station breaks and found us stayed with us.

I took personal charge of every crucial detail: for example, making sure that the limousines were provided on time; assigning sorority members from UCLA to each participant to make sure nobody got lost on the way to the bathroom; I assigned someone to sit in a person's seat when he or she was called on stage to present or receive an award, thus avoiding having empty seats in the theater. Attention to detail is the key to being in charge of your life. That philosophy sure paid off for me at the American Music

Awards Show. We've out-rated the Grammys consistently, and we did that from a standing start with no previous experience in running an award show.

Taking charge also means knowing who are your friends and who aren't. I have had countless contacts with people in the entertainment industry. Naturally, there are many favors exchanged in this type of business. So, over the years, you end up owing and being owed some big ones. But then comes the time when you want to collect. I have been a very generous purveyor of favors over the years, and so, when I need help, I can call on many people. There have been some notable exceptions.

I live by a combination of the eye-for-an-eye principle and the turn-the-other-cheek doctrine. I'll turn the cheek once; the second time I take the guy's eye out! When I had to put on the first American Music Awards show, I called in a favor owed to me by a friend. He had let me down once before and I had accepted his reason. This time, he found another reason for ducking out. Now, I didn't offer another cheek for him to slap. I made a mental note not to be there when he needed me in the future. Since then, the wheel has turned several times, and when I was in a position to help him I sat on my hands.

I learned many years ago that there are two sides to every person: the loving and generous side that we all take pride in; and the aggressive side that our religious teaching and cultural conditioning has told us is evil.

I strongly disagree with the belief that aggression is synonymous with sin!

Without the tough side of my nature, the loving side of me would have to retreat into hiding. After numerous disappointments, even the most generous giver would begin to feel used, cheated by life, and would withdraw into seclusion, disappointed that there are "so many bastards out there." I, instead, make the bastards out there duck for cover when they act rotten so that the generous side of me can continue to feel free to show itself. Maybe that condenses down to a new version of the Golden Rule (Dick Clark arrangement):

"Do unto others as you would have them do unto you, but don't forget to protect your ass at all times. And take whatever measures that are necessary to ensure that."

Taking charge means being a man or woman of action. It also means judging and being judged by what you do, not by what you say. Most people say things that they firmly believe to be true about themselves. Their words define what they would like to be, not what they really are.

If you assess what people do, not what they say, you will always be closer to the reality of what they are. If you follow this principle, you will make few mistakes in judging people in business, in friendships, in marriage, and in life.

Taking charge doesn't require a special gift. You need only to be convinced that you have arrived. You are an adult, fully qualified for life and must be prepared to use all your endowments to the fullest. I have succeeded in life using this simple philosophy, and so can you.

4

Building Your Team

Let me lay to rest one misconception about success. Let's bury, for all time, the concept of the "self-made man." It takes many people to make one person successful. Nobody can do it solo. If you want to be the most successful nurse, your patients and the doctors with whom you work must help you achieve that goal. If you have designs on being the best high school teacher in the state, your students had better get the grades to prove how good a teacher you are. If you want to make a fortune with a business idea, your employees have to produce quality goods in large numbers. Also, your potential customers must be convinced that you, rather than your competitors, deserve their patronage. Making it in any field is a team effort. Nobody can do it alone. I learned that early in my career, and the lesson keeps being reinforced with every step up the ladder I take.

To make it big, you have to learn how to build, and hold onto, a loyal team. You must become a leader. You must inspire and marshal the efforts of other people toward a goal you have designated. Through my experience, I have identified several crucial aspects to achieving this:

1. The team must see their destiny as united with yours.
2. Each member of the team must trust you to fairly represent them.
3. You must be able to identify the strengths of each member of the team and enhance these— encouraging people to grow, constantly.
4. Each time you meet a crisis, you must go back to the team and renew your mandate, making sure they are all on your side at critical moments.
5. You must recognize that your role as leader is different from your role as "person." As their leader and representative, people have a right to regard you differently, to hold higher expectations of you than they would if you were their peer.

After signing the lucrative NBC contract, I knew that I would have to substantially augment my production staff. I wanted to maintain high quality in all my existing shows and, at the same time, to fulfill my dream of doing a big live T.V. variety show. I was in a bind of my own creation: how to cope with the success I had wrought without compromising my standards.

Kari and I sat down and surveyed the territory.

"Dick, we have quite a few really talented people on our staff, but few have had significant experience at handling major responsibilities on their own," Kari said, touching on our vital lack. We had young, keen people on our team, but most of them were used to receiving supervision. Now, under the new contract, the quantum leap in my good fortune would have to be matched by a major increase in responsibility and hard work by many young, inexperienced people. I was willing to reward them financially for their increased efforts, but would they feel up to the new tasks? That was the crucial question raised by Kari.

"What about Jim, for example? He came into my office last week asking for a raise. The guy deserves more, but not for doing the job he's now performing," I told Kari. "Do you think he can take on a big chunk of our new action?" I asked, feeling in advance that her answer would be yes.

"Jim's biggest problem is his lack of confidence in himself," Kari confirmed. "He's an ace, but he doesn't believe in himself."

"I think he needs some shock therapy," I concluded, and Kari agreed.

I called Jim into my office and began, "I can't give you the raise you asked for."

Indignant, he replied, "Why not? I've done a great job for you. Why you yourself commended me on my work only last month."

"That's true. But the job you do could be done by a well-trained chimpanzee. It's repetitive and leads nowhere. It's certainly not worth more than I'm now paying you. My compliment on your work was sincere. But I think you're capable of far more, and I won't give you a raise until you show me greater initiative and creativity."

I could see Jim's face turn red after my chimpanzee remark. His eyes looked inward as I discussed the idea of creativity and initiative. He seemed to be scanning himself internally, asking, "Do I have the qualities that Dick is looking for?" Recognizing his uncertainty about his own capabilities, I offered him a chance to prove himself. "Jim, you know that we're facing a big challenge. We're growing up as a production company, and you have to grow up with us. I want you to take on a new area of responsibility that I know you can handle," I said, outlining his new responsibilities. As I spoke, he seemed to become increasingly insecure. I felt he needed a jolt. "In conclusion, Jim, it's put up or shut up from now on. Either you show your stuff, or you look to be someone else's chimpanzee." I could see his face flush with anger, although he tried to hide it behind a veneer of compliance.

"Let me think it over, Dick," he said.

"Don't take too long. We have a big job to do, and it won't stop for your deliberations," I said, keeping up the pressure.

After that conversation, I heard through the grapevine that Jim was looking outside the company for work of the same type he had been doing for me. There were a few offers made to him, but not for more than I had been paying him. He was boxed in; he could either choose to grow, or he would stagnate at that level in his career. Jim chose growth.

"I decided to take you up on your offer, Dick," he announced, bouncing into my office a few days later. "When can I begin?" he asked.

"Right away," I answered, taking out some papers and explaining his new tasks to him. Since that time, Jim has made giant strides. He's learned to function as an entrepreneur and has gone off into multiple deals that have brought him and my company substantial gains. He doesn't even look the same. His aura of confidence is unmistakable as compared to his obvious insecurity of just a few years back. The key to his transformation was my ability to show him that his destiny could be linked with mine. He accepted my invitation to join the growth team. Now he's one of my leading lights. Building your team means helping people build their own careers in complementary ways to your own. Self-made men help many other people make it, too. The benefits of other people's growth accrue to the team-builder.

Having gotten my staff organized for the big push—the NBC contract meant many new projects had to be gotten off the ground right away—I headed back to New York for some tapings and some new business ventures I was exploring. When I arrived, my assistant confronted me with the news that an old friend of mine, someone whose identity will have to remain anonymous (let's call her Jill), was having a nervous breakdown. Life had gone sour for this talented woman and she just couldn't cope. She had made a suicide attempt and failed. I rushed to see her at the hospital.

Looking up at me from her bed, tears in her eyes and a tube protruding from her nose, she said, "I'm sorry, Dick."

"For what, Jill?" I asked.

"I know it's crazy, but I feel I fucked up by not making good, even at trying to kill myself. I can't do anything right anymore, not even suicide," she said, beginning to sob.

"Goddammit, Jill, it makes me angry to see you treat yourself like a piece of crap!"

"Give me some evidence that I'm anything else," she retorted, some anger in her voice. "One marriage after the other has failed. I was a winner but couldn't keep my career on track. I have finally collapsed, like I knew I would years ago. I always felt that all this success was a great act I was putting on and that everyone would finally see through it. Now it's happened—the game is over."

"If I didn't love you," I said angrily, "I'd turn you over my knee and spank you, tubes, intravenouses, and all. When are you going to take your own talent seriously? When are you going to take your life under control and realize that you are not destined for the garbage heap like you feel you are?"

"I have no reason to believe otherwise, not since I was a kid, Dick. I had a miserable childhood. By some lucky stroke, Nature gave me a voice which has made me some money; but as a person, I don't have the right makeup. I'm a bust."

"Prove to me that you're a fuck-up," I challenged her.

Startled, she asked, "What do you mean?"

"Appear on my show and prove that you just can't do anything right anymore," I challenged her.

"I can't, I can't . . ." she said, starting to sob all over again.

Outside her room, I met her manager, an old friend. "Bob," I said, "I want her on the show next month."

"How can you say that, Dick? Have you gone soft in the head? You know I love the kid and want the best for her. If she fails you, she'll kill herself. Next time, she'll succeed. I can't let her do it," he insisted.

"How long have you known me, Bob . . . twenty or more years? I've never wanted anything more than having her appear on my next show. I know she'll be a smash. I'll give her the backbone she lacks. Do it for me," I implored.

"Even if I wanted to say yes to your insane request, I wouldn't be able to convince her to appear," he explained.

I replied, "All I ask of you, Bob, is to tell her that I invited her on the show and you gave your word that she would appear. I'll take it from there, okay?"

Bob assented. When he announced her forthcoming appearance on my show, she went berserk, calling me from her hospital bed.

"I won't . . . I can't do it, Dick. You can't ask me to do it; have a heart."

"Look, Jill, all the arrangements have been made. The publicity has been out for days. You've got to do it. Bob gave me his word," I insisted. Jill agreed, although fearful and reluctant. I knew that this was more than a gamble on whether one act or one show would work. I was playing with Jill's life. Bob had been right in his projection; failure for Jill would have been the last straw. She'd surely try suicide again and, perhaps this time, would succeed. Yet, to let her continue to wallow in her past failures was a guarantee of disaster. I preferred to take the chance that my confidence and her talent would be a winning combination. Bob entrusted me with the greatest treasure he possessed: his love for Jill, the most important performer he had ever managed. Bob felt confident to let me do what he could not: to rebuild Jill's confidence and her career.

Trust is not easily won. It takes years to develop and is consolidated through many experiences wherein the other party sees your honesty and your competence *in action*. Bob banked on those years in our relationship. I had never once let him down or deceived him. But this time the stakes were higher than ever before. Jill's life and Bob's eternal conscience were at stake. I could not fail them.

Six times prior to the show, right up to the moment she was to go on stage, Jill asked and pleaded to be replaced. I refused. To affirm her belief now that she couldn't make it would be disastrous, especially after she had ignited a small, feeble spark of confidence—enough to make her appear at rehearsals. I steadfastly refused to allow her to back out of her commitment. The show went on.

At her cue, I had to literally shove her out on stage. After Jill had taken two halting steps from behind the curtains, the audience went into an uproar at the sight of her. Her back straightened as she walked into the spotlight. In a hoarse voice, she took the microphone and said, "It's good to be back." The audience gave her a standing ovation even before she sang one note. When calm was restored and she began to sing, I saw the phenomenon that was Jill come back to life. I couldn't hold back my tears. Neither could

Bob. I hadn't failed him or Jill. I couldn't have felt more gratified in my life than I did at that moment.

Kari asked me after the show how I could have taken that big a risk with such confidence. I replied, "I have one great advantage: I've built my career on inspiring others to do great things in show business. I made my name by helping other people to make theirs. My strength, over the years, has been in helping other people realize how good they are, not how great I am. Jill is a gold mine of talent, and I'm the best miner there is."

Jill has since started back on her way to the top. I will always have her on my team because she and Bob can never find a more loyal person than me to have on theirs.

Kari and I were working furiously now to get enough projects off the ground to satisfy our NBC contract. We were into movie-making for television in a big way, but my heart and mind were still riveted on my lifelong ambition: to do an Ed Sullivan type of live variety show. In my opinion, the epitome of good showmanship is in presenting consistently excellent live entertainment. More than any other ambition, I had to realize this dream in my lifetime. I asked Kari to give this project top priority, and she came to my side with all her considerable vigor. We were determined to put together the finest talent ever fielded for the "Dick Clark Variety Show." And then I got the news.

"There's been a change in command at the network," said my assistant. "Fred Silverman has been named President of the network and is Chief of Operations over all aspects of programming, *et cetera . . . et cetera. . . .* Do you think he'll kill the variety show as he did on ABC?" asked my aide.

"I don't think he can kill it outright, but he can see to it that it dies of its own accord," I warned. "Let's call a staff meeting this afternoon and get everyone geared up for an awfully big crisis."

I have learned over the years that the best way to face major changes and crises in my organization is to bring my staff into my confidence. I act as if I'm not the leader of the organization in perpetuity. Instead, I run for re-election (at least in my mind) each time a major event arises.

I want my staff to realize that I want their support and their approval to lead them through each crisis. They, in turn, have an opportunity to re-elect me (in their minds) as their leader to face each imminent crisis. The tactic of going back to renew popular support on every major issue is one I learned from skilled politicians.

If you are elected to a six-year term in the Senate, and you act as if the public no longer exists once you take office, you will never win another term. In fact, you may be impeached. (Ask Richard Nixon about the advisability of taking the people you lead into your confidence in times of crises—perhaps he has learned a thing or two since Watergate). In my organization, I ask my people to line up behind me each time a major crisis occurs. I don't assume arrogantly that, just because I pay their salaries, they will automatically show me allegiance. When Freddie Silverman surfaced as NBC's President, my staff needed the opportunity to vote for me once more, especially on the issue of the "Variety Show." I entered the meeting room, which was buzzing with energetic conversation and alive with speculation.

"I have been informed that the 'Variety Show' has been slotted for Wednesday. All of us know how important it is for this type of show to be aired on a Sunday in prime time, as was 'The Ed Sullivan Show.' We have a serious problem here, not of our making. I won't quit now. I still want to give it a shot, even though the odds have been stacked against our success. I called this meeting because I wanted to know how everybody else felt about the situation. If you want to work on something else, that's okay."

The room remained hushed for a moment, and then one of my younger staffers spoke out: "Me, walk out on a hit show—are you kidding?" she said, while all of us swallowed hard. She knew, as most of us did, that we were doomed before we began by the placement of the show on Wednesday night.

Her declaration of loyalty was heartwarming. It was soon echoed by everyone in the room. Not one person asked to be transferred off the project, even though it looked like it was destined for failure from the moment it was assigned a Wednesday night time slot. My staff remained loyal and devoted, as they have through the years. That's because I'm that way to them. I care about them and never take their support for granted. They back me up and always take my devotion for granted. That's the way it is if you want to be a leader. If you want to survive in life, you have to be known as a durable friend, colleague, and leader. I wasn't prepared to turn and run in the face of insurmountable odds. I offered my staff the opportunity to leave the ranks and they refused. We all went down together on that show, but they knew me to be a survivor; they stayed with me and we all have risen to even greater heights since that failure.

That meeting, where my staff showed their loyalty, gave me a powerful feeling that I must have done something right in my life to have won such support from those around me. My pride was boosted at a time when I most needed it. As I walked down the corridor back to my office, my assistant chased after me, shouting, "Emergency phone call, Dick! You can take it in my office.

Years back, at another moment of business crisis, I had received another urgent call. At that time I had raced to the phone, my mind reviewing a blinding parade of potential disasters. None of my fears was as bad as the news I had gotten from a disembodied voice at the other end of the line. "Mr. Clark, this is Dr. Shapiro. I have bad news for you. Your mother has passed away. I'm so sorry. . . ." I couldn't hear the rest of the detail he was reviewing about the fatal illness that finally claimed my mother's life. I felt momentarily like a child—an orphan. I wept as I walked home. Losing my mother provoked more acute sadness than I have ever experienced. The emotional ties to her went back to birth. Her comfort formed the basis for my deepest layer of confidence. Could I survive? Would I survive this loss? I was flooded with emotions and memories, unable to summon reason to my side during the time of my mourning.

On the way to her funeral, I was stopped by a person on the street. "Mr. Clark, I admire you so much. Could I have your autograph?"

My entire equilibrium was momentarily shaken. I had retreated back to my family roots during the mourning period, completely forgetting about my other self—the Dick Clark of my adult life. My first impulse was to say, "Get lost, lady. Can't you see I'm going to my mother's funeral?" I held back, however. Something in me said: "How could this innocent person know about your grief? She's just responding to the person you led her to believe you are *at all times*—Dick Clark, celebrity; Dick Clark, the guy who's got it all together. Don't blame her for seeing the person you've tried so hard to create, even though you're dying of depression at the moment."

"Give me your book, ma'am. I'll sign the autograph. What's your name?"

5

Making It

Putting together a major production in the movies or television draws from every resource a person has available. Aside from the endless problems, the overwhelming responsibility, and the huge financial risk, there is the overriding issue of reputation. One big bust and the road back can be a long, arduous one. Because of the high visibility of my work, reputation and track record mean everything.

As you follow the careers of many celebrities, you'll notice that they move, as I did, from entertaining to producing and directing. Have you ever wondered why an established, big-money star would want to hassle with the plumbing of the behind-the-scenes business when he or she could demand a big fee for just acting and then take the money and run, win or lose, as far as the movie is concerned? The answer—for me, at least—is craftsmanship. It's true that getting into the behind-the-scene phases of show business is lucrative. But a major motivating force has to be the desire of a talented person to gain control of the whole works. The true craftsman wants to manipulate all the tools of the trade to come out with the best possible finished product. Making the *whole thing* work is the driving force behind the real artisan.

To make it, you must be an uncompromising craftsman. And you must have a track record of success, time after time, if you want anyone to want to invest money, time, or their own reputation in your products. When I ask a network or movie house to show one of my films, I'm asking them to put their livelihood on the line. People have to respect your reputation if you want them to follow your banner. That's why people in highly visible fields, such as show business, work so hard at their craft and also guard their reputations—sometimes with the help of a phalanx of public relations advisors.

Once you've made it, you acquire not only wealth, but a public image of success that follows you around wherever you go. There are numerous instances in my personal life when I regretted being the "Dick Clark" everyone expects him to be.

I recall, right after my divorce, sinking into a deep, blue mood. Like so many people, fresh from the trauma of a failed marriage, I asked myself: "What's out there for me?" And then I answered, "Nothing . . . absolutely nothing." Hurt and disappointed, I was reluctant to expose myself to any more pain.

My friend Al would have none of that defeatism. "Dick," he began in an imperious tone, "we're going out on the town tonight. You've had enought time to wallow in self-pity. The world is waiting for your comeback."

"No, Al. I'm just not ready yet. Give me a few more weeks," I pleaded.

In a knowing tone he replied, "That's what they all say, Dick. I won't take 'No' for an answer. I'll be by to pick you up at eight. We'll go to dinner and then hit a few bars."

"All right," I agreed weakly.

My mind wandered all over the map. I recollected my recent severe disappointment in a failed marriage. I felt like kicking myself for failing to notice earlier how sick the relationship had become. "Had I known just a few years back, maybe I could have turned it around," I thought. Then I caught myself, remembering that Al had just warned me about wallowing in self-pity, exactly what I was doing with my endless post-mortems of the relationship. I set my jaw and made up my mind to be brave tonight. My mind veered way off course to an episode in my youth.

I had been a shy kid who, after some early social failures, had found myself. I became President of the school, was into many extracurricular activities, and had no problems getting enough dates. One girl, however, intrigued me. She was special in many ways. Her mind was more alive and perceptive than any other in the school. She was able to get right to the point, penetrate your defenses in an instant, but never in an embarrassing way. Her laughter was infectious and uplifting. She was really special. She was also a dwarf.

After struggling with myself about it for many weeks, I decided to date her. All the "What will everybody say . . .?" comments I anticipated couldn't dull my enthusiasm to take her out on a date. I called her and she eagerly accepted my invitation.

We went out on a regular high-school-type date: from the movies, to the local greasy spoon restaurant—jukebox and all. I went to school the next day in a high mood, proud that I had acted on my instincts about that wonderful girl. None of the kids who had seen us together the previous night passed any nasty comments. They, too, respected and admired her, despite her physical stature. My friends were grateful and proud that I had had the guts to enjoy the best aspects of her without holding her size up as a false measure of her humanity. Looking in the mirror to straighten my tie, I saw myself smiling in remembering that very special date. Just then, Al rang my doorbell and I knew it was time to face the big, cold singles world. Somehow, I felt that it was going to be all right. I knew that I would be judged on who I really was and not as the person that "Dick Clark" had become publicly. That expectation couldn't be further from the truth.

Going to a singles bar as a celebrity has its advantages, up to a point. Imagine yourself at any place in the world, with people in the room, who are familiar with your face and willing to accord you immediate recognition. That's what it's been like for me for the past twenty-seven years. It's a great asset, in a singles bar, to walk in and be known instantly. There are no awkward moments of glancing around, looking to catch someone's eye, then measuring the meaning of the reciprocal gaze. "Was that an interested look?" you wonder. "Did her eyes say yes or no?" you think, as you rehearse what your first words will be. You walk over, heart pounding, and introduce yourself with the usual, "Hi. Can I buy you a drink?"

As a celebrity, these awkward introductions are immediately circumvented. The women approach you and they say, "You're Dick Clark, aren't you?"

"Yes. And what's your name?"

"Candy," says the gorgeous redhead in tight French jeans.

"Where are you from?" I say, feigning interest, when I'm really wondering what it'll be like to make love to another woman after having been faithful throughout my entire marriage.

"I'm from Beverly Hills," she replies.

"Nobody's from Beverly Hills," I correct her.

"Really. I was born right here in L.A. and went to Beverly Hills High School," she says with some defensiveness in her voice.

"Okay, I believe you. Say, are you interested in going somewhere quieter?" I ask.

"Sure," she answers excitedly, running over to her friend to tell her she'll have to get home by herself and thrusting a set of car keys into her less fortunate companion's outstretched palm.

Over in another corner of the bar, Al has been watching the action like a protective older brother. He winks at me and simultaneously raises his glass of white wine in a mock toast as I leave with the luscious redhead.

We drive directly to my apartment, since, immediately after entering my car, she puts one hand on the nape of my neck and the other deftly opens one of my shirt buttons. She inserts her hand into the opening to stroke my chest as I nervously try to start the car.

At the apartment, she wastes no time undressing to get to the task at hand: "making it with Dick Clark." I realize, this first time with a woman other than my wife, that, while I was slumbering in married life, the sexual revolution had indeed arrived. She makes all the moves, does all the seducing, and looks very eager to carve out one big notch on her garter belt for having made it with a celebrity. Not as confident and able to get into sex on a knee-jerk basis as she is, I try to slow down the action with some conversation.

"Tell me about yourself," I say, regretting my comment moments after it is uttered, since it opens the floodgates to a string of confessions and opinions that completely turn me off. It turns out that this woman is the heiress to a fortune; she is an adherent of the women's movement but is only able to make one contribution to the cause—not shaving under her arms; and she gets uncontrollably turned on by men from Ireland, preferably blue-collar workers.

Now, I have nothing against any of the things she stands for. Taken individually, they are laudable. I admire blue-collar workers. They are the true backbone of this country. I love the Irish, especially their friendliness. I respect Gloria Steinem and all her counterparts in the women's movement. I even like Beverly Hills and many of the rich people who live there. But, somehow, I can't put these all together in one person and get turned on. Regrettably, in spite of her fabulous physical endowments, flaming red hair, and infinite libido, I am unable to become sexually aroused. Undaunted, she takes out a joint and lights up. I have never done drugs and am unwilling to start now, so I refuse her hospitable offer of a "hit." Never to be thwarted, she offers to do anything kinky I may have ever wanted to do but was afraid to request of a fair damsel. This only makes me want to retreat even more. Seeing her victory slipping away from her and fearing the morning's question from her friend, "Was he really good . . . did you turn him on?," she begins to weep. That calms her frenzy and my fears and we make glorious love all night long.

The moral of this story, believe it or not, has relevance to making it big (that's not an intentional play on words). A producer of successes has to create a coherent final result out of many individual components. This woman, despite her beauty, had a total image that was a jumble—a confused mess that was a turn-off. My high school friend—a dwarf—had it all together. She knew how to combine her physical appearance, her personality, and her attitudes into a winning combination. If you want to be a winner, you must take all your assets, put them together in a way that makes the whole more than just a sum of the parts, and then make the entire end result work! Whether you are a redhead from Beverly Hills, a diminutive high school girl, a housewife from Detroit, or a celebrity producer, you have to be conscious of the way the parts are put together to make the whole. That's the key to making it big, in bed or in business.

Over the years, I have had a string of major successes. Some are very obvious ones, such as the durable "American Bandstand" show, which has become a true institution. "The Twenty-Thousand Dollar Pyramid" show has been on the air for seven years—not a bad track record for a fickle business like network television. But, in many of my proudest current achievements, few people know of my contribution, unless they bother to read movie or television credits as they're flashed across the screen.

I produced the *Elvis* movie for television and, in a total turnabout, ran it successfully in theaters all over the world *after* it had had its first run on T.V. I've been involved in producing dozens of winning projects for T.V. and theater showings, the latest being the Beatles movie, of which I'm proud. Getting this type of an act together is a monumental challenge—the kind of thing that turns me on and gets my juices flowing.

When I consider how any of these projects came up winners, it all comes back to that same principle: make the whole greater than the sum of the parts. The thing has to work! That's the creative challenge. From the business end of it, to an analysis of the potential impact it will have on an audience, the project has to make sense.

In putting together the *Elvis* movie, Kari and I had a monumental task to accomplish. First of all, the Elvis phenomenon has been beaten to death. There are Elvis T-shirts, Elvis look-alikes, Elvis baby carriages, Elvis memorial statues, Elvis everythings-under-the-sun . . .

and more. How do you do a movie that will not further debase the image of a truly great performer? How do you select an actor to play the role who will not come off looking like a pallid imitation of a charismatic superstar? What part of this man's life story do you tell? Too much glorification and you end up with a comic-book depiction, not a real, live human being. Revelation of his seamy side—and we all have skeletons in our closets—would look like, and would be, cheap exploitation. And there has been more than enough of that in Elvis's case.

I went over numerous scripts, adjusting, splicing together strong parts, cutting out weak or inappropriate ones, doing reconstructive surgery on a story that few writers knew as well as I did. Finally, a script was handed to me at the eleventh hour. The writer asserted that this was the "final draft" and urged me to go ahead with the production, which was now running into potentially costly delays.

I put my life on "hold" and squirreled myself away to review the script. Time was really running short. Any more changes would cost hundreds of thousands of dollars, as the entire production crew was assembled and on the payroll, work or no work. I read and frowned, read some more and frowned some more. This wasn't the Elvis story I wanted to tell. I exploded out of my room and burst into the writer's office.

"You've got three days to re-do the entire thing," I started, provoking unsuppressed gasps and murmurs. "I want you to bring in a story that tells about the man as well as his accomplishments. I want to portray both the Elvis the people know as well as the Elvis who they are unfamiliar with—the youngster who had a dream and made it come true. How did Elvis get to be 'Elvis,' as we all knew him?

That's the question I want answered in the movie. Got it?"
I asked.

I had to make my point emphatically—there was no
more time to spare. "Remember, three days—no more!"

I left the room, convinced that he would live up to the
challenge. I had selected him carefully. I wouldn't have it
any other way. I had confidence that he would rise to the
challenge. But first, he had to know the urgency of the
situation, and I, as leader, had to drive that point home.

The response of the writer to this situation confirms a fact
I have always known: Parkinson's Law works both ways. As
you may recall, Parkinson's Law states that "a task will
expand to occupy all the time available for its completion."
Everyone interprets this very valid principle in one direction only: if you have more time to waste, you'll waste it for
sure. Most people use Parkinson's Law to rationalize their
failure to produce more. I use the same law to get people to
increase their productivity. If the law says that, whatever
time you give someone to finish something, they will
complete it by the deadline, then I can contract the deadline to its briefest realistic limits and expect results. It
worked in the *Elvis* movie script. The writer brought in a
marvelous revised final script, done exactly how I had
wanted it, in just under three days. Thank you, Mr.
Parkinson.

After the production was successfully completed, I had
the joy of seeing it break records in the ratings on television. But I was committed to going further than that. I had
worked out a worldwide theater distribution deal, fully
expecting the movie to be a smash hit at the box office, too.
It was, but not without some complications.

Because Elvis was such a legendary figure, it was easy to
exploit him. Many ruthless entrepreneurs did so, even

while his body was still warm. That disease tried to attach itself to my movie, as I knew it would. I had cautioned my staff to be on the lookout for unscrupulous people who would try to make local hay out of the showing of the movie. Each town in which it played could be watched, according to my plan, to ensure that the movie would be presented as a work of art—something the critics have agreed it is—and not as another Elvis exploitation. Despite my careful precautions, one local promoter tried to cash in on the fact that he was going to present the film in his theater. My staff detected his plans in the nick of time. But I don't like close calls.

I assembled my crew of experts and we analyzed how this near-exploitation could have gotten as far as it had without detection. My language was indelicate but effective.

"I want each of you to operate as if you were surrounded by idiots and that you, and you alone, were entrusted with the duty of watching out for them. Furthermore, even though the situation has been corrected with the distributor, I want someone to call and bust his balls. The message has to be delivered, about this movie and every other project with which we're associated, that we respect our work, and so must the people who show it to the public."

The word went forth from that meeting. We defended the quality of the presentation of that film as carefully as we had prepared the story itself.

To make it big, every part has to work, from conceptualization, to execution, to impact. I have always been a person sensitive to audience reaction. That's the nature of my work. Every aspect of the total operation must be carefully thought out and implemented. What's true of movie production is true of every other field.

- You wouldn't want to fly with a pilot who was great at takeoffs, a terrific navigator, but a screw-up when it came to landing the plane.
- Would you buy a house from a contractor who put in the finest paneling in the den but skimped on the roof and foundation?
- In your marriage, will you succeed if you are great in bed, are the world's best parent, but humiliate your spouse at parties?

To make it big, you have to be on top of every detail, and, also, you must put the pieces together artistically. All the parts (not just the ones you favor) must be coordinated to make up the final masterpiece! That's the key to making it big in any field and in any relationship.

My greatest successes have all had that one thing in common: I am involved in every phase of the operation, constantly coordinating the overall result to bring about the desired impact. The dials that I try to read are the tastes and sensibilities of the public who watch and, hopefully, enjoy our work.

I operate, on stage or behind the scenes, as if I'm playing to one person: you. I never see a host of faces out there. That's terribly confusing and dulls the senses. It's like watching the Vietnam War on the seven o'clock news and concluding, from the casualty statistics, that you know what it's like to have been there. When I look at a television camera, I see one person: you. When I read a television script, I act as if I am your elected representative—a member of the audience, not a television producer. When I walk into a crowded boardroom to negotiate a multi-million-dollar deal, I see the entire assemblage of people as one: just a person out to become a success through creative hard work.

Surviving has not been a magical process for me. It is no different for you. The rules are:

- Make all the parts work together.
- Be fussy about selecting the right concept before beginning a project.
- Pay close attention to the details of all phases of the implementation.
- Never take your eye off the impact your actions may have on the other person, whether that's a person in the audience, a business associate, or someone you meet in a singles bar who turns out to be a celebrity.

6

Bouncing Back from Failure

Even though we suspected before it went on the air that the "Variety Show" was going to fail—the Wednesday night scheduling of the show having sounded its death knell—my staff and I were determined to put on the best live entertainment that was ever seen on T.V. We were professionals. We had to do our best for our own ego's sake. The pressure of working under the cloud of defeat finally got to one of my staffers.

Marge was thirty-two years old, an attractive brunette whom you'd have thought, on first glance, was a model or actress. She was incredibly bright and creative—the kind of talent that would have been wasted just smiling in front of a camera. Instead, she had wisely decided to become a production person—a less glamorous but more mentally challenging end of the business. One day, one of my assistants came into my office and meekly said, "Dick, I feel like a rat, but, for her own good, I have to tell you that I think Marge is really getting strung out on drugs. Could you talk to her? She admires you. Maybe you'll be able to help her."

I called Marge into my office. She gracefully slid into a chair and cocked her head in a slightly defiant and coquettish way as I began. "Marge, I hear that you want to be the first woman to fly across the Atlantic . . . on Quaaludes. Is that correct?"

Caught off guard by my directness, she made a slight feint and then came right to the point. "I don't know what you mean. . . . Oh, what's the use of trying to wiggle out of this? You already know, or else I wouldn't be here."

"True. However, If I didn't think that you were a colossal talent—someone worth saving—you would have already received your final paycheck and I would have been spared the unpleasant duty of putting you on notice because of the drug thing."

"Is that it? Is it 'shape up or ship out'?" she asked, somewhat skeptical about my resolve.

"That's *exactly* it," I emphasized. "But one more thing: What's the problem? Why the need to neutralize your brain twenty-four hours a day?"

"Life is shit. I feel that I'm going nowhere. At school, I used to be full of enthusiasm. Looking down the road, I visualized a life of excitement and achievement. After one failed marriage, a couple of rotten relationships that threatened to be replays of the marital disaster, and a career that is nine-tenths drudgery to one part creativity, I feel it's all over," Marge said, tears beginning to well up in her eyes.

I began to recall her earlier behavior, and it fell into a pattern. Marge had always seemed like the perennial college girl. She would talk about "the good old days" at length but rarely would reveal much about her current life. Even her dress and attitudes seemed arrested at an earlier epoch—her idealized college years. I asked, "Marge, what do you look forward to? What are your current dreams, your options for the future?"

"I can't think of any," she sobbed as she buried her face in a collection of Kleenexes she had drawn, one by one, from the box on my desk.

"You've stopped growing. Instead of constantly renewing yourself, you've tried to play out one role—the gifted collegiate—and have found it unsuited to the rest of your life. Can I help you learn to play some other parts? Would you give me a chance to show you how to be a production executive?" I urged.

"You haven't given up on me, Dick. I appreciate that," she said, pulling herself together.

We had made contact. I offered to be her mentor for a time. She accepted playing the role of growing daughter: to learn, from my example, how to move forward on multiple tracks, constantly renewing herself to ensure survival. I had learned that strategy the hard way.

My life, on the surface, appears to be as smooth as a mountain lake at sunrise. Since the payola hearings many years back, there has been hardly a ripple in my career. Practically all my shows have been sold-out successes. Even the canceled "Variety Show" made money. From afar, you'd conclude, "Lucky guy. He's never been down. He doesn't know what it feels like to make a comeback."

That assumption couldn't be more incorrect. For every success, there have been twenty false starts. Each victory has been the end of a trail fraught with hardship. I've succeeded by adhering to several principles:

- As many times as I'm knocked off my feet, I have to get up, brush off the dirt, and start again.
- Adaptability is the key to survival. In order to bounce

back from failure, I must keep growing to adapt to the new realities of my life. Failure is a statement of my inability to recognize a pitfall. Once I've fallen, I make it a point to identify the trap so that it will delay me only that one time.

- I am concerned with the present far more than with the past and future. My perspective is primarily the here-and-now. I dedicate my energy to capitalizing on the opportunities at hand. That's where progress is made.

- Like a running back in football, I always keep my forward momentum going. The brilliance of O. J. Simpson and Jimmy Brown was their ability to instinctively move forward, even when off balance. If you're going to fall, make sure you gain an extra yard before you hit the ground.

As I set out to be Marge's mentor—to teach her how to bounch back from failure—I recalled the major reverses of my own life.

At the peak of my early success, I learned that my wife and a "good friend" were having an affair. I was destroyed. Pleading for her to reconsider didn't work. She seemed intent on throwing out the life we had built and trading in "Dick Clark" for a man who worked in a Midwestern steel plant. My fame and fortune could do little to offset the emptiness she felt in her life. I had been deluding myself for years thinking that we were happy. I was too preoccupied with my work to recognize the emotional bankruptcy of our relationship. I took the loss hard and foolishly.

Alcohol seemed a natural escape. Drinking was an acceptable part of celebrity status. I had ample opportunity to go out with colleagues to "discuss business," and to use that occasion to tank up and numb my senses. That pattern continued for some months until a buddy pulled me up one day with the remark, "Dick, you have a drinking problem."

"No," I replied, "I have a shitty life. Booze helps me tolerate it." Although I was trying to rationalize my drinking, I couldn't ignore his frank statement. Nobody had ever told me straight out that I had a drinking problem—or any other sort of problem, for that matter. I was "Dick Clark, All-American, clean-cut boy," or so said my press releases. How could *I* be depressed, rejected by my wife, and a drunk to boot? Nobody but my friend dared to confront me with reality. I wanted to resist his assertion, but the power of the truth was greater than my ability at self-deception. I made an immediate resolution to combat my loneliness by finding another woman. That was my second mistake.

Rather than learn from my failed marriage—study where I had gone wrong and try to shore up those aspects of my personality—I decided to recoup my loss immediately. The first woman I met who was kind to me became my second wife.

After only two years, we were both miserable. We knew the marriage was over then, but neither of us was able to end it. She was more realistic than I. My second wife asked for a divorce on several occasions and I begged her to reconsider. She gave in, to the detriment of both of us. We suffered in the relationship for seven more years until neither of us could stand the loneliness any longer. My third mistake was holding onto a failure out of fear of admitting my mistake.

- I had run from the recognition of my first marital failure through the use of alcohol.
- I had escaped the necessity of analyzing and learning

from that mistake by quickly and blindly entering another relationship.
- I had clung to the second failure in an attempt to delude myself that it could be "turned around."

Finally, I took stock of my life. Perhaps it was because I sat down one day and projected ahead to when the kids would be grown and realized: "I'll be in my fifties when the kids are on their own. Do I want to spend the best years of my life waiting for them to grow up? What would be the better contribution to their lives:

- Remaining in a dead relationship in order to be able to contribute to their lives on a day to day basis?
- Getting out while the children were still growing up and showing them that I could solve my own life problem, even if it meant not being in the same house with them?

I opted for the latter. The children and I have never regretted that decision. After I had established a new and satisfying relationship with Kari, the kids began to partake of my life.

I had learned a hard lesson in my two failed marriages. I would never again allow myself to stagnate. What security had I purchased by clinging to two failures? Of what benefit was it to anyone for me to have delayed the inevitable for so many years? My marriages taught me to keep growing and learning at all times.

It's become fashionable nowadays to talk about the mid-life crisis. When Marge came into my office, defeated by life at age thirty-two, I guess I could have attributed her dilemma to the mid-life crisis. But she was hardly in the mid-life era. She had let her growth become arrested at the college level. I had allowed my personality to stop growing at the stage of becoming well known on "American Bandstand." After that success, I thought I had it made. I assumed that everything I would do in the future would turn out successfully, including getting married and raising kids. Marge had had the same erroneous belief; she felt that her college successes had launched her on a trajectory to lifelong stability and satisfaction. Both of us were dead wrong!

Getting a good start in life is a definite asset. But making constant mid-course corrections is essential, even after the most successful launching. Otherwise, you'll shoot for the stars but will end up lost in outer space. Realizing that you have ended up in that limbo is what's called "The Mid-Life Crisis." Its remedy is achieved by:

- *Re-evaluating your goals.* Ask yourself if where you are heading is relevant to who you are at the present. You mustn't just keep plodding ahead on a trajectory set in your youth until you are so far off course that you can't find your way back. You must constantly re-assess your goals.
- *Re-evaluating the strategies you are using to get to those goals.* What was a smart thing to do yesterday may be dumb, inappropriate, or destructive today. Only a small amount of wisdom is timeless. In a growing person's life, most wisdom becomes obsolete in a few years and must be replaced by updated principles which apply to the new realities you constantly encounter.
- *Recognizing that the only chance you will ever have to grow will arise out of a recognition of your deficiencies and mistakes.* It's so easy, when stuck in the doldrums of the mid-life crisis, to convince yourself that the

answer to your problems is to quickly chuck your job, marriage, and way of life and replace them with shiny new models. The pain of stagnation is so great that it can cause you to thrash about and be seduced by the first glimmer of relief—be that a new relationship, job, or possession. Unfortunately, that "solution" is usually the old problem in disguise, as my own experience taught me. During the mid-life crisis, you must take the past, analyze its weaknesses, and effect a solution that works. The lessons learned in that past, bad experience are your best insurance of future success.

- *In putting your new life into action, you must recognize the need to make constant readjustments in order to get to your goals.* Nobody is so clairvoyant that, once they set a goal, they can go straight to it unerringly. What happens, in reality, is that you encounter new and unanticipated obstacles each day. You may have to change strategies or establish a new and more realistic goal.

Surviving the mid-life crisis requires you to look at the short years ahead without going into a panic. You mustn't stampede ahead, pressured by the feeling that "time is running out." Instead, you should use your previous experience to greatest advantage, recognizing who you are, what type of life you need to build, and then (acting as if you have all the time in the world) set out to build a new life. You'll end up doing the job well and in a minimum of time. I know it can be done because I made all the mistakes in my own life and then, in my mid-forties, got smart and did it the right way.

I spent many hours with Marge. I had to encourage her constantly at first. Years of stagnation give a person the feeling that forward movement is impossible. Then, when a little bit of momentum is finally achieved, the person gets frightened that "things are going too fast." After all, in comparison to a living death, any movement at all is experienced as unstable and uncontrollable. I had to get Marge to recognize that she was beginning to grow again, and the price she would have to pay for this was to give up the familiar and secure.

Marge started to get involved in relationships again. At first she made many mistakes. She would attribute qualities to men that they didn't have. She saw in them the answer to her needs, rather than recognizing what they really were; I, too, had made that fatal mistake. I cautioned her to go slowly and be experimental. Each relationship reveals a different facet of your own personality. It is as if each other person is a mirror which reflects you from a different angle. After seeing yourself reflected in many of these mirrors, you start to learn who you really are.

Marge's new life of rediscovery and renewal began just as our "Variety Show" reached its end. It was ironic that her rebound, under the tutelage of her mentor, would soon have to be emulated by the mentor himself.

The final word that the show had been canceled came on my birthday. I was angry. A special force welled up inside me. It felt like a mixture of outrage and sadness. I saw my dream of twenty-five years vanish in one decision. I had come within two rating points of success, despite the odds against our success from the very beginning. The powerful emotion inside me grew.

"Should I blame Silverman?"

"No," I thought. "What good would that do?"

"Was my staff at fault?"

"Not at all. They were loyal and hard-working right on through," I recognized, gratefully.

My reflexes came into play: "I have to sit down, analyze this debacle, and make sure that this kind of thing never happens to me again," I concluded. "The best thing I can do is learn from this experience and try again some other time."

Even my calm reasoning and re-appraisal could not stem the emergence of a growing tidal wave of emotion. I wanted to cry, scream, strike down the people who had undermined me . . . and, at the same time, I wanted to hide, rest, and renew my spirits. My mind was in conflict. Images of all my past losses cascaded uncontrollably through my consciousness: my brother's death . . . the death of my mother . . . heartbroken after Brad died . . . the first divorce . . . the second failed marriage . . . and, now, the death of the "Variety Show," my lifelong professional dream. Sadness kept fighting for center stage but was being repulsed by an even stronger emotion. That insistent usurper of my consciousness felt like anger but was not. It was my powerful survival instinct, sharpened and energized by past experiences, and now at my disposal once more. I sat down at my desk, alone in my New York apartment, and began to plot the way back. "All that counts now is getting up again," my mind kept repeating. The words of encouragement that I had given to Marge during these recent months still echoed in my brain. "Keep going . . . find new avenues . . . learn from this defeat . . . grow stronger from this lesson . . . find a new world to conquer . . . and never give up!"

Kari and I threw ourselves into multiple new projects with renewed vigor. One success followed the other. My greatest problem in the coming months was that everything I was working on started to sell *all at once*.

Movies . . . television programs . . . commercial business deals . . . the takeover of the Westchester Premier Theater—project after project began to come up a winner. I had survived again. Even the biggest disappointment in my career had failed to torpedo my drive and enthusiasm. An inner force had carried me from a childhood in Mount Vernon, to my early radio experience in Utica, to a new beginning on T.V. in Philadelphia, where I found fame and fortune, and finally to L.A., where my production company came into its own. My survival instinct had once again come to my rescue. I had overcome failure and was back again on the road to success.

7

Staying on Top

What were you doing twenty-seven years ago? Do you remember? Had you reached your peak? In my case, way back then in the Fifties, as a man in my early twenties, I had already made it to the top. During all these intervening years I've remained successful. If there is anything unique about my career, it's got to be my staying power: my ability to survive. I'll match my endurance record with anyone from Muhammad Ali to Johnny Carson to Billie Jean King. My expertise, aside from show-business know-how, is in the tactics of survival.

Most people adopt the wrong strategy for success. They look for ways to get into the charmed circle, totally ignoring the endurance factor—the strategies that will keep them there—once they arrive. I'm no one-term President. Neither should you be a flash in the pan.

One of the most important principles you must learn to live by is that life is a marathon, not a sprint. If you try to go full tilt from the outset, thinking only of the finish line, you may get there first, but you won't stay on top, or you'll collapse as soon as you break the tape. What is the secret of the winning marathon runner? How does he or she manage to keep up the pace for so long?

Think back to your high school track-and-field meet. Remember your mental set when you were running the hundred-yard dash? I'll bet you had only one thing in mind: breaking that tape at the finish line. Nowhere in your thinking was there any room for a review of the condition of your body. Would your muscles get sprained . . .? Would you run out of wind . . .? The sprinter ignores all these considerations. They can be dealt with some other time. Right now, you've got to beat the other six guys to the tape!

The marathoner has a different mental attitude. He or she doesn't like the grimaces of pain on the face of the sprinter. Those tortured expressions tell the marathoner that the sprinter is forcing the body past its limits—a dangerous excess that will take its toll at a later date. The marathoner is perfectly right. Have you ever known of a sprinter who won his or her event in two successive Olympics? I can't recall one. Sprinters all burn out in a few short years. That's because they don't really prepare for the long haul. The name of the game is short-term fame, not long-term endurance and repeated success.

The marathoner, in contrast, takes constant readings of the internal condition of mind and body:

- "I'd better watch out not to get dehydrated."
- "Stay loose . . . make sure not to pull a muscle."
- "Let the other guy sprint on by. I'll pass him a few miles up the road when he's winded."
- "Got to keep that mental attitude right. I'm starting to tense up emotionally. I need to get into a good mental space. Maybe thinking of a pleasant scene or inhaling

the smell of flowers as I run by them will lower my stress."

The marathoner is a self-monitoring, self-regulating bio-system: a machine built for endurance, with lights flashing mentally to alert the chief engineer that attention needs to be paid to one or another of the sub-systems which make up the total winning machine.

In my life, I have been the classic example of the marathon runner. I constantly tune in to my inner state: both mentally and physically. Although I'm not a health nut, I'm appropriately health conscious. For me, that means yearly medical check-ups; regulation of my nutri-tion; an awareness of my emotional state; and a constant review of my total growth as a person.

By paying strict attention to all these aspects of my life, I stay mentally young, healthy, and have the energy to stay on top.

The sphere of medical care is a blind spot for most people. How the heck can a layman judge the quality of a doctor's work? Yet, the necessity of having the best medical advice is crucial for everyone, and especially for the super-achiever. If you want to live on the ragged edge between top performance and over-exertion, you need to have the best medical consultants on your team.

I use a simple system for obtaining excellent medical care. First, I treat my family doctor as a medical broker, as well as a professional who dispenses first-line care. By that, I mean that my family physician is the clearing house and coordinator of all the information and data concerning my health. If I see an eye doctor, my family physician gets a copy of his report. When Kari visits her gynecologist, our family doctor gets a report of his findings. The focal point of our entire health protection program is the growing file on us kept by our family doctor.

In medicine, the situation is no different from in my field—television production. In my business, it would be disastrous if the right hand didn't know what the left hand was doing. If my cameramen needed one type of film for a movie and my purchasing department went ahead and bought something else because they could get it at a good price, a calamity would occur. The filming would go sour or the project would undergo costly delays.

Where my health is concerned, imagine how serious things might get if one doctor was treating me for headaches, while another one was giving me medication for ingrown toenails, and the two drugs, when combined, caused convulsions. That's not a fantasy of disaster which my mind concocted. It's a realistic medical possibility. And, yet, few people appoint anyone to coordinate their entire health care program. How the heck can you win a football game without a quarterback? How can you remain healthy without having one person in charge of coordinating your entire program of health protection?

The next thing I do is carefully select the specialists who treat my family. Now, that can be a confusing task, because the reference points most people use are wrong.

"If I were you, I'd use Dr. Harris for your gall bladder operation. He did such a wonderful job in Julie's operation."

The self-styled expert recommends a doctor on the

merits of his work, *as she judges it!* And what are her criteria? Hearsay, nothing more.

I have a simple way of picking a specialist. I ask my family doctor, or friends of mine who are physicians, which doctors they use to treat members of their own family.

"Hey, Charlie, when your mother had her gall bladder taken out, which surgeon did you call in?"

My friend Charlie, an allergist, is part of the medical fraternity. He knows who keeps up to date and who doesn't; which doctor has had more than his share of complications; how much each surgeon drinks; how careful the specialist is, in and out of the operating room; and which of his colleagues are nine-tenths hype and "bedside manner."

In fact, many doctors have told me that the profession operates like a private club. Doctors associate in cliques, referring back and forth to each other for friendship rather than medical reasons. Dr. A refers all his surgery to Dr. B because they are tennis partners, not because he thinks Dr. B is the best surgeon around. But when Dr. A's mother or wife needs to have gall bladder surgery, you can bet he picks someone who is handier with a scalpel than with a tennis racket. So my rule is: "Ask your doctor who his doctor is." It's a safe bet you'll connect up with a competent physician.

As you may imagine, I have quite a hectic schedule. It takes me from L.A. to New York at least every ten days, with London and other cities around the world thrown in once a month. Naturally, I get a kick out of my work, including my travel; otherwise, I wouldn't do it.

During the course of one week, I go out to the most expensive and elegant restaurants several times; then I subsist on pizza and fast foods the other days. I, like many other people, eat in unpredictable patterns and often on the run. Yet, I try to keep my nutrition in balance.

In my opinion, nutrition is a frequently overlooked aspect of health care. Your doctor tells you that your body is like a machine that needs periodic maintenance and repair (done by him at his prices), but then he ignores the fuel that runs the machine—your nutrition.

Food is your only energy source. Yet, few of us pay as much attention to what we eat as we do to the type of fuel and grade of oil that we put in our car's engine. Consequently, many of us have personal "energy crises," running low on needed fuel in our bodies, even though there are abundant supplies of it all over.

You wouldn't put Chivas Regal in your gas tank just because it's expensive and it will burn. Similarly, I don't assume that, just because food is expensive and exquisitely prepared, it constitutes a good fuel for my body. In fact, I think that many so-called "junk foods" are just as nutritious as the fare served at gourmet restaurants.

Since your personal physician may be ill equipped and poorly motivated to monitor and advise you on nutrition, I suggest that you learn about it on your own, or consult a qualified nutritionist. Assess your habitual eating patterns; analyze your diet's deficiencies in vitamins and minerals. Then take the appropriate supplements daily. Probably more health protection can be gained by good nutrition than by any other readily available means.

Part of my awareness of nutrition is a concern with over-nutrition—gorging myself on food to the point of overweight. Kari and I both love food and, God knows, we can afford to eat the best. How do I stay slim under those circumstances? I do that by *not* following the Ten Commandments of Obesity.

I'll bet you didn't know that there were a second set of tablets brought down from the mountain by Moses. Those were the Ten Commandments of Obesity—all the rules for becoming and staying overweight. More people obey these commandments than the set governing morality. I make it a point to break all these rules and stay thin. The Ten (Fat) Commandments are:

I. *Thou shalt never feel hungry.*

The fact is that thin people always feel hungry; only fat people are constantly satiated. When your body sends out hunger signals, it tells you, "Hey, give me some food to burn."

My response is, "Go eat some of my fat, instead." The hunger remains; the fat gets burned off.

II. *If thy spouse eats at the same time as you do, the calories cancel each other out.*

Isn't it funny how two people can delude each other into believing that it's all right to overeat, as long as your mate does so at the same time. It's as if they believe that "by encouraging my spouse to overeat, those calories will counterbalance mine"—a sort of subtraction phenomenon. The only thing that gets canceled out when you get your mate to overeat with you is your guilt feelings. The weight gets unloaded from your conscience and goes straight to your hips.

III. *Thou shalt end each meal by eating something sweet.*

There are many people who eat carefully all during a meal and then blow it by eating a thousand-calorie dessert. On this point, I am severe with myself. I dole out sweets to myself like Scrooge. My body is thankful for this parsimony.

IV. *Thou shalt eat when mealtime comes, whether hungry or not.*

What is it about time that makes it so dictatorial in some people's lives?

"It's Thursday and we haven't made love three times this week. Don't you think it's time to get it on?"

"The clock struck twelve noon. It's time to eat."

The only reason for eating or making love is that a need exists that should be fulfilled. The time to eat is set by your body, not by the clock. Eat only when you must, for the sake of nutrition, not because the clock struck twelve.

V. *Thou shalt diet tomorrow to compensate for thine indiscretions of today.*

Isn't it a pity that tomorrow never comes? So many good things would happen if only tomorrow would come. The garbage would get taken out; the term paper would get finished; the check would be put in the mail; and the weight would be lost through careful dieting. Alas, tomorrow never comes, so you have to diet today . . . and today . . . and today . . . and every day of your life. That's what weight control is all about.

VI. *Thou shalt not get on the scale the morning after a food orgy.*

What a great thing information is in helping you run your life. Scientists know that you can't beat accurate, timely information for getting to the root of a problem and solving it. The same goes for your accountant, your doctor, and your lawyer. Give them good information and they will all do a great job of protecting your interests. But, in the sphere of dieting, some of us act as if the opposite were true: "Don't give me the facts. It will be easier on my conscience that way."

After an eating binge, you must get on the scale to see how much damage has been done. In fact, you should get on your scale every morning like clockwork to make sure that you know just exactly how much food you should allocate to yourself that day. Only by keeping extremely close tabs on your weight can you hope to control it.

VII. *Thou shalt not leave food on your plate.*

Finishing everything put on your plate, just because it's there, would be sensible if you had carefully analyzed exactly how much food should have been served in the first place. Unfortunately, most portions are served without such scientifically precise consideration.

"A hunk of meat, a ladleful of soup, and a scoop or two of mashed potatoes will make a good hearty méal," you conclude. Now, you'll lose weight if you eat a metric "hunk" of meat, but not if it's just a plain, old-fashioned "hunk." In fact, did you know that the average, old-fashioned "hunk of meat" has as many calories as a loaf of bread?

Because you're not apt to precisely measure and weigh your food before eating it, when you feel satiated, stop eating! The children in Europe no longer go hungry. It's no sin to leave food on your plate.

VIII. *Thou shalt eat to counteract boredom.*

Isn't this an all-too-common trait—eating because you're bored? In fact, many couples gear their entire social life around food. "We'll go out to dinner with the Bradys; then, after the show, we'll go to this great little place for dessert."

What would happen if you decided to eliminate food from your social life? Would you have any friends left? If not, then your way of socializing needs some major surgery. If you don't separate socializing and eating, you'll never get your weight under control unless you move to Antarctica.

If you eat to counteract boredom, get right to the root of the problem: join a club; take up a new hobby; engage in a sport; have an affair. Do something, but don't eat!

IX. *Thou shalt try every new fad diet that comes on the market.*

I know dozens of people who are dieting experts. They have tried every diet from Scarsdale to Duke University; from low fat to high water; from grapefruit to eat-all-you-want-and-throw-up-a-lot. They are the diet virtuosos. They are also among the fattest people I know.

Weight control is a way of life. It starts in the supermarket, where you have to exercise good judgment. If you bring home that quart of chocolate ice cream, you'll certainly gain weight by the time it's consumed. Keeping your weight in line is a constant discipline that should be as important to you as is your financial well-being. Looking good and being healthy costs nothing; in fact, you save money by not eating. You can look like a million dollars, even though you don't have that much money in the bank.

X. *Thou shalt keep a set of "fat clothes" at the ready at all times.*

The sign of an episodic dieter (which, translated, means: "a usually fat, but sometimes thin, person") is the possession of a "fat wardrobe." Having a second set of clothes for your other identity—the obese one—is a declaration, in advance, that you expect to lose the war of the waistline.

If you take my advice, next time you get your weight to the ideal level, have a bonfire with your "fat wardrobe." Destroy your other identity forever. "Burn your britches behind you." You won't be sorry. You'll stay thin.

Keeping my weight down is important to me, as a show-business person; I'm sure you'll agree with that. Why do you think that it's so crucial for me to look good? I'll bet that, if you saw an overweight television host, you'd say, "That guy's got problems. He can't get it together with his weight. I'll bet he can't get it together anywhere else, either." If that's what you'd believe about me as an overweight television personality, people must also think that about you when you're overweight.

To stay on top, people must respect you and admire your ability to keep trim and fit. Your weight is a walking advertisement of your ability to show self-discipline and good judgment. If you look good on the outside, people will be more willing to respond to you in everything else you do. That's a fact of life!

A critical aspect of my power to survive and succeed is the way I use my emotions. It may be old-fashioned or totally unscientific, but I believe that God gave us emotions for a purpose. They were certainly not meant to be hidden, suppressed, or ignored. I use my emotions as a special asset in my life. They are guideposts for measuring how I'm doing.

- If I'm sad or depressed, I know that something is missing. I look for ways to make up the deficit, and that usually eliminates the depression.
- If I'm tense or anxious, I know there is an overload situation in my system. I don't stubbornly press on, ignoring nature's signal to ease up. Instead, I take off—usually for a long weekend—and coop up someplace where absolutely nobody can find me. Then, with batteries recharged, I'm more capable of figuring out what tripped the circuit breakers in the first place. I tackle each situation one by one and get over the crisis.
- If I'm angry, I know that something is standing in the way of my need for satisfaction. I don't fume, curse, and shout pointlessly. I blow my top, but then I harness the energy release to get positive results! Anger is a natural force that can either explode and destroy, or it can be channeled in the service of building solutions to your problems.
- Guilt's a great emotion. It keeps order in our society. Unfortunately, in some people, it keeps a little too much order, and in others, too little. Mrs. Jones, guilt ridden since her strict religious childhood upbringing, makes an obsession of orderliness. She's neat to a fault; she never stops dusting, vacuuming, and spraying the house with disinfectant. She is tormented by guilt feelings for having had an impure thought. Her

neighbor down the street has too little guilt. She doesn't even flinch or have a nightmare about sleeping with Mrs. Jones's husband.

When God gave out guilt, He forgot to use His measuring cup. So Mrs. Jones got an overdose and her neighbor got too little. You can correct that.

Next time you feel guilty, ask yourself: "What crime did I commit?" Remember that only in Russia can you be found guilty of thought crimes. In a free society, your guilt is determined by what you do, not what you think.

After you have identified a source of excess guilt, ask yourself: "Since it doesn't belong to me, whose guilt is this? Usually, you'll find that the guilt originated in an erroneous childhood belief: something you were told by your elders but, because of your young age, didn't fully comprehend. After you re-assess the guilt, you'll find that most of it can be discarded.

If you want to make it to the top and stay there, you'll have to re-evaluate your guilt feelings many times. We revere people who are leaders—the self-made men and women who made this country great. At the same time, our religious and cultural attitudes revile the *desire* to get to the top. Our schizophrenic national morality tells us that the end is great; the means stink! You can go nuts following that logic.

As someone who has made it, I'm never shy about my success or ashamed about the way I've achieved it. My greed (if you call it that) to acquire wealth is healthy. Money is a thermometer of my success and a tool for achieving more of it. I'm not shy about admitting that.

Keeping in touch with your emotions is a necessary task

for someone who wants to make it to the top and stay there. I use the information contained in my emotions to my advantage. That data is the most accurate, fastest, and most reliable informant I have about my condition as a person. I will never ignore or tune out the words of wisdom given by my emotions.

A critical lesson I've learned over the years is that I must keep growing at all times. Stagnation is living death. What's worse, it causes things you treasure to die, as well: like your marriage, your career, and your sense of dignity.

Constant growth is the only way for me to go. That's why I re-evaluate my life at frequent intervals, set new goals, and constantly renew myself. Obsolescence is an affliction of people, as well as of machines. When a drill press becomes old-fashioned and inefficient, you can scrap it. When your way of life becomes obsolete, you can either discard it and design a new one, or you'll end up on the scrap heap yourself. I prefer the former solution.

Kari has been a great partner for me, not only because she is such a giving and responsive person, but also because she is a *growth partner*. We love to learn new things together; take on big projects in tandem; go wild at the same time. Our lives are totally experimental and constantly undergoing renewal. That way, we have grown in the same direction and our compatibility has been enhanced over the years.

When we lost the "Variety Show," Kari knew I'd bounce right back. She was tuned in to where I was at. She saw me going off in twelve directions at once and joined me in this whirlwind, knowing that work and success would be the best antidote to depression.

I know many couples, otherwise well matched, who break up simply because they can't get their growth phases in sync.

Charlie wants stability when Joan is in an active phase of growing. She wants to go back to school. Charlie says, "What the hell do you need that for? Don't we have a good life? Haven't we been to Europe twice in the past three years? Look outside: Isn't that a great piece of property we own? Why the heck do you need law school?"

Charlie fails to recognize that Joan is in the grips of the virus that infected him only five years earlier when he was seized with the need to learn how to fly. She chided him about becoming the neighborhood "Eddie Rickenbacker," and he resented her insensitivity. "Damn it," he used to think to himself, "why doesn't she realize that I feel stagnant? I need a new world to conquer, and learning to fly has been a lifelong aspiration."

Regrettably, there are too many Joans and Charlies. In fact, four of every ten marriages end in divorce nowadays. And, in my opinion, it's due to one single cause: growth failure—or, more specifically, the inability of the couple to learn how to synchronize and complement each other's growth needs.

In order to stay on top in life, you must learn how to grow constantly. You must also facilitate your partner's growth. With the two of you working at it together, both of you will stay on top.

Scanning back over the past quarter-century of my life, I identify the marathon runner in me. I feel the pulse of my physical health. Without a sound body, no achievement can be sustained. I monitor my emotions to give me early warning of impending problems. As soon as I read the signals in my moods, I take corrective action. I fuel my body with the proper balance of nutrients, knowing that an energy crisis can bring everything to a halt. I attempt to keep my forward momentum going as a person. Constant renewal of myself means that I will be in shape at all times to meet modern challenges.

My need to win has the strength of an addiction. But it's a healthy addiction called "living life to the fullest."

8

Remaining Eternally Young

What do you think of when you hear my name or see my face on T.V.? I'll bet you think about my youth. "How does he stay so young looking?" most people reflexively remark about me. To me, a youthful appearance is not as important as retaining a young state of mind. By that, I'm not referring to being "a perennial teen-ager," as some people have assumed. There are special attributes about youth that deserve preservation for a lifetime.

My concept about growing up is that we add layers of wisdom and experience to those that already exist. We don't go through a molting process, shedding everything that came before and replacing our identity in toto.

What's so special about youth? What are the attributes worth keeping? Here are my thoughts:

- Young people are too naïve to be defeatist. Hence, they are willing to take on any new challenge with the attitude, "Why not me? Why shouldn't I be the one to succeed?" Their adult counterparts reason differently: "Why me? What's so special about me that I should be the anointed one?" Give me youthful enthusiasm and confidence any day. I'd rather be a naïve person, struggling to win, than a "wise" defeatist.

- Deceit is a skill we acquire with age. Honesty gets young people in trouble. It's also one of their most appealing traits. Ask any man who's ever dated a much younger woman what attracted him. You'll usually hear: "Her honesty and openness. My wife and I lived together for twelve years and never got through to the core of each other as well as I've been able to do with ————." (Fill in the blank with the names of a multitude of women who are ten to twenty years younger than the wife.)

  To be honest requires a special bravery that youth possesses more of than adults. "If you reject my honesty, that's your problem," is the youthful attitude. Full-grown adults are too concerned with security: hanging on for dear life. Hence, they make too many compromises; they forgive and forget too many times; they hide their true feelings and turn the other cheek until the partner gets bored with their martyrdom.

  Be brave and honest. Speak your mind like a young person. Your mate will appreciate your candor and it will keep your relationship young.

- Young people are not refined, thank God! I believe that most adults get caught in a refinement trap—a narrowing of tastes and attitudes that, through the years, closes them off to most new experiences. With the exception of food, many adults cease experimenting with their lives. They get used to a type of clothing, a circle of friends, a certain kind of music, and a set of moral circumstances. Everything new or different is considered beyond the pale of good taste. That's why adults adapt to social change less readily than their children; that's why the hope for emancipation of disadvantaged groups lies in the blending together of flexible youth, not "refined" adults.

• Young people love to participate in fads. We adults revile them for their suggestibility. Yet, there is something about fads that is of value.

If you talk to a university professor, you may hear that: "Washington is funding projects that have to do with energy and cancer research. Those are the 'hot' research areas." Fads exist in the scientific community, but scientists are not disparaged for following them. Researchers who get big grants to study cancer aren't considered slavish groupies.

Following the current of the times is a necessary survival skill. In business, it's called "having a responsive marketing program"; in science, it's referred to as "grantsmanship"; and in the youth culture, we call it "following a fad."

• "Youth is always demanding too much freedom." That's the war cry of most parents who have teen-aged children. What is "too much freedom"? As parents usually define it, it's anything the teen-agers want to do that they haven't yet done, or that can't be observed by the parents as it's being done. Ask the teen-ager about this dilemma and you'll hear the plaintive cry: "They won't give me freedom until I've developed responsibility. But how can I prove I'm responsible unless I'm given more freedom?" Good question!

The same Catch 22 situation exists for adults: How can you grow unless you take risks and attempt more than you're comfortable with or capable of? The drive of the teen-ager to move forward with his or her development is too strong to resist. The parents give in reluctantly and chew their nails as their children go out in the world and learn how to master its difficulties.

Many adults would do well to emulate that teen-aged risk-taking spirit. There would be fewer failed careers and broken marriages if adults would lunge ahead into the unknown like their teen-aged children, saying, "Don't worry. I'll figure out how to handle the problems when I meet them."

Constant renewal is necessary for survival. You must be free enough to grow, brave enough to take risks, and confident enough to believe that everything will turn out all right.

Evolution has taught us about survival of the fittest. It has also shown us how the only species that have not become extinct are those with the capacity to adapt to a constantly changing environment. Freedom to roam, experiment, and change is a guarantee against becoming extinct over eons or even in one lifetime.

If my life, I've raised three children. All of them have made that hair-rising journey through the teen-aged years. They've had it more difficult than most kids because their father was a nationally known celebrity. More was expected of them, and they, in turn, expected more of me than I was able to give. For one thing, I wasn't home constantly. They were raised primarily by their wonderful mothers—my ex-wives. Yet, we have remained extremely close. One of the reasons for that is our honesty in dealing with each other. Another thing that binds us together is my positive regard for them. I expect the best of them, and they live up to my hopes.

It would be easy for me to give these children the finest clothes, racy sports cars, and bank accounts brimming with money. In fact, most people assume that I have done just that. To the contrary, I have told my children, "Don't wait around for my money. You're as smart as I am. Go out and make it on your own." My kids get the same kind of cars as yours: a used Honda is good enough to drive to high school. My children work for their allowances and have learned that dignity comes with achievement. I expect my kids to be capable. I'd be the last one to rob them of the opportunity to prove themselves just because their father happened to be "Dick Clark." As a result, they have never disappointed me.

Raising children is a marvelous experience. The hidden benefit is that it gives you an opportunity to recycle your own childhood at every stage of theirs. The mistakes your parents made in raising you—the events that stung—will be revisited as your children reach the age of your childhood traumas. You'll be reminded of unfairness, losses, battles, and frustrations. All those problems you weren't able to solve in growing up will be confronted again as your children mature. Now, however, you can bring your adult intelligence to bear on the problems. As an adult, you are free to do things your way. The leftover parts of growing up that weren't accomplished because the circumstances weren't right for it in your own childhood will now be completed as you raise your children to maturity.

It's appropriate that my story should end where it began. My youth, a period when I catapulted to success, has never been lost. By staying eternally young in spirit, I have survived a half-century of severe personal losses and business reversals. Yet I've been able to rebuild and constantly move forward. Youth gave me my beginning in show business. Youth has been my trademark. Staying young has been my secret survival strategy.

APPENDIX

A Comprehensive Survival Workshop

EXERCISES FOR CHAPTER 1

How to Get Set and Take Stock

Playing Chess with Your Life

As you can see, in my life I have had to face formidable adversaries—people who wielded great power, and situations fraught with the possibility of failure. Whenever I confront such a situation, I adopt the strategies of a chess player:

1. Know the rules of the game.
2. Think several moves ahead of your opponent.
3. Make unconventional moves to keep adversaries off balance.

Complete the following series of questions and answers to help you learn how to play chess with your life and stay moves ahead of your problems:

1. Define your chief roles in life (for example, wife, son, boss):

    (a) _____

    (b) _____

    (c) _____

    (d) _____

2. Describe two rules which determine your success or failure in each role (for example, as a wife: *Rule 1*—I must be my husband's best friend; *Rule 2*—I must try to look attractive):

(a) Rule 1_____

Rule 2_____

(b) Rule 1_____

Rule 2_____

(c) Rule 1_____

Rule 2_____

(d) Rule 1_____

Rule 2_____

3. What are the principle objections others have about how you perform in each role (name two complaints other people have had of you in each role)?:

(a) Complaint 1_____

Complaint 2_____

(b) Complaint 1_____

Complaint 2_____

(c) Complaint 1_____

Complaint 2_____

(d) Complaint 1_____

Complaint 2_____

4. What constructive changes can you make to overcome each complaint?:

(a) Change 1_____

Change 2_____

(b) Change 1_____

Change 2_____

(c) Change 1_____

Change 2_____

(d) Change 1_____

Change 2_____

5. What are the greatest problems you will face in each role in the next five years (specify two problems for each role)?:

(a) Problem 1_____

Problem 2_____

(b) Problem 1_____

Problem 2_____

(c) Problem 1_____

Problem 2_____

    (d) Problem 1_____

         Problem 2_____

6. What can you do *right now* to head off each problem?:

    (a) Remedy 1_____

         Remedy 2_____

    (b) Remedy 1_____

         Remedy 2_____

    (c) Remedy 1_____

         Remedy 2_____

    (d) Remedy 1_____

         Remedy 2_____

7. How can each role be changed to make it more satisfying and likely to lead to success?:

    (a) _____

    (b) _____

    (c) _____

    (d) _____

8. Who would object to these changes, and why?:

    (a) _____

(b) _____

(c) _____

(d) _____

9. How could you deal with each of these objections?:

(a) _____

(b) _____

(c) _____

(d) _____

10. Which one of the roles you perform in life is most important to you (remember to identify that role which gives you the greatest ego boost, not the one that society or the family values the most)?

11. If it became necessary, which role would you sacrifice or compromise in order to succeed in your most important role?

12. How would you react to sacrificing one of these roles?:

(a) _____

(b) _____

(c) _____

13. How would you deal with these reactions?

(a) _____

(b) _____

(c) _____

14. How would others react to these sacrifices?

(a) _____

(b) _____

(c) _____

15. How would you deal with the reactions of others when you sacrificed one role in order to succeed in another?

(a) _____

(b) _____

(c) _____

Making it in life means thinking steps ahead of your current situation and planning for all the contingencies which may arise. Your reactions and those of others have to be anticipated even prior to embarking on your journey to success. Otherwise, you will be undermined by your own attitudes or those of others as you shake up your life to produce rapid forward progress. The exercise you have just completed will help you take an advance look at the obstacles to your success. By planning in advance to overcome them, your chances for survival will be greatly enhanced.

Building Your Life on Strengths

Did you ever hear these remarks?:

"I can't do that. I might screw up and then I'd be in a mess."

"I'll give you a dozen reasons why this deal won't work out."

"I don't mind betting. I just can't take losing."

These remarks and others like them are the hallmarks of losers. People who know how to identify only their weaknesses will back away from success and head directly for failure. It makes common sense, doesn't it, that if your mind is focused on your weaknesses, you'll base your actions on those? Whereas, if you tune in to your strengths, you are apt to use them in dealing with life. If you're worried that you'll drive your car off the side of the road and can't take your eyes off the ditch, that's where you'll end up. But, if you rely on your ability to steer, you'll stay in your lane and get to your destination.

To survive, you have to take an inventory of your abilities and rely on those in a realistic way. I learned, in my early life, that I couldn't be like my brother. However, I had unique strengths that I could use to get to the top. What about you? What are your chief assets? Take the following test to identify your major strengths:

1. What is your most effective intellectual tool?

    (a) Reasoning power   ☐
    (b) Foresight   ☐
    (c) Curiosity   ☐
    (d) Ability to track detail   ☐
    (e) Creativity   ☐

2. How do you use this strength in each important aspect of your life?:

   (a) Career   _____

   (b) Relationships_____

   (c) Recreation   _____

3. What could you do to more effectively and extensively employ this strength?

4. Why haven't you done this yet?

5. How do you react to people emotionally? To define this aspect of your life, name one person toward whom you feel each of the following emotions:

   (a) Love   _____

   (b) Hate   _____

   (c) Disgust   _____

   (d) Admiration _____

   (e) Guilt   _____

   (f) Shame   _____

   (g) Fear   _____

6. Do you have trouble expressing any of these emotions?

   Yes ☐   No ☐

   If yes, why do you feel uncomfortable with this emotion? Identify a safe situation in which you can practice expressing this emotion (such as rehearsing a confrontation with your boss by telling your wife exactly what you would like to say).

7. Name the three people with whom you have had the longest relationship:

(a) _____ (Years_____)

(b) _____ (Years_____)

(c) _____ (Years_____)

8. When was the last time you saw each of them?

(a) _____

(b) _____

(c) _____

9. If you haven't seen or spoken to any of these people within the last month, why haven't you maintained this relationship? How can this be remedied?

10. Why have you had success at work (name the three attributes or contributions that have brought you success to date)?:

(a) _____

(b) _____

(c) _____

11. What are your plans to capitalize on these abilities?:

(a) _____

(b) _____

(c) _____

12. Do you think you'll ever reach your career goals?

Yes ☐   No ☐

If no, cite three reasons why you won't make it:

(a) _____

(b) _____

(c) _____

13. What are you doing now to get around each of these obstacles?:

(a) _____

(b) _____

(c) _____

14. What were your favorite hobbies as a teen-ager?:

(a) _____

(b) _____

(c) _____

15. Have you given up on any of them? Why?

16. What can you do now to resume these activities that gave you so much pleasure in years gone by?

If you take an inventory of your life, as the above test will help you do, you will find strengths in many places:

- In your intellectual abilities
- In your emotional capabilities
- In your relationships
- In your career
- In your hobbies and pastimes

Each of these vital aspects of your life can reveal assets which can help you succeed and survive. I turned a childhood interest in entertainment into a lifetime, lucrative, and satisfying career. As a person who knew my strengths, I was able to bet on myself and win. If you learn to analyze your life and extract from it your greatest strengths, you will be a good bet for survival and success.

EXERCISES FOR CHAPTER 2

How to Set Out on Your Journey to Success

Life Planning

I'm sure you'd never set out on a long trip without taking along a road map. It would really spoil your vacation if you had reservations at a hotel in Florida but got lost and ended up in Tennessee. Yet, so many people who are otherwise deliberate and careful set out on their life's journey without any planning at all. Then, when they get lost, they further confuse the issue by blaming their failure on bad luck or the malevolence of other people.

From the outset, you must have a life plan if you hope to succeed and survive the disasters along the way which could thwart you. But how does a person construct a life plan? Since it's impossible to predict the future, how can people draw up a map of their destiny?

Nature has given us one remarkable ability that makes this task possible—the capability to dream and fantasize. I place great value on dreams. They are not mere illusions which I dismiss as impractical. In my experience, the mind's forecasting capability is revealed by its dreams and fantasies. Even children are capable of doing a swift and accurate assessment of their abilities.

During childhood, your mind converted this information into a dream or fantasy. Naturally, as a child, dreaming was all you could do with your assets and liabilities. You weren't capable yet of translating them into a career plan with practical steps to get you from A to Z. But growth and motivation can make that dream into a reality, provided you don't let it die or ridicule it until it hides in embarrassed silence.

In my life, the earliest dream I had for my future was to be an entertainer. Lots of kids have the desire to go on stage and become famous. With the death of my brother, I had a special impetus to realize my loftiest goals. Brad had been a hero, and I felt impelled to live out a grandiose destiny in his honor. I clung to my dream and it provided guidance for me throughout life.

What are your dreams? What can you do to revive them and bring them to fruition? Take the following test and find out.

1. As a child, who were your heroes?:

   (a) _____

   (b) _____

   (c) _____

   (d) _____

2. What attribute did you admire in each of them?:

   (a) _____

   (b) _____

   (c) _____

   (d) _____

3. Which of these attributes do you possess?

4. Why have you abandoned trying to develop the others?

5. What can you do to revive those attributes and goals you admired but abandoned?

6. If practical issues didn't stand in the way, what would you like to see changed in your life?:

   (a) _____

   (b) _____

   (c) _____

   (d) _____

7. Write a brief paragraph about how your heroes from childhood (or someone with special abilities which you don't possess) would get around the obstacles in order to make the improvements necessary in your life.

8. How can you develop the abilities to make these changes? Do you possess them now but ignore or not rely on them?

9. Select one of your childhood heroes whom you would most like to emulate. Name three reasons why you have been unable to get where he or she has gotten in life:

   (a) _____

   (b) _____

   (c) _____

10. Of these reasons, which are due to a personal lack, and which are the result of external factors (such as bad luck or not being in the right place at the right time)?

Personal Deficiencies	*External Factors*
(a) _____	(a) _____
(b) _____	(b) _____
(c) _____	(c) _____

11. Now describe one method for improving each personal deficiency and one way around each external obstacle. If you can't think of the solutions yourself, name a person you can consult who would know the correct answer for each problem you face:

Growth Solution to Remedy Personal Deficiency	*Detour Around Obstacle to Life Goals*
(a) _____	(a) _____
(b) _____	(b) _____
(c) _____	(c) _____

11. Why haven't you already implemented these solutions?

Starting the Motor

Once you have revived your dream, you have to make major changes to attain it. Shaking up your life is always stressful. In order to go forward to your goal, you need to be able to withstand the uncertainty and tension which you will encounter.

It wasn't easy for me to leave a secure job as a newscaster in upstate New York and move to Philadelphia. I was frightened and lonesome for home. Yet I knew that I had to position myself closer to the mainstream if I was ever going to attain a measure of success in my career. I had to deal with depression resulting from the loss of my family and friends whom I had left behind; cope with loneliness; deal with new challenges in my profession that I, at first, felt ill equipped to handle. All these factors caused me a great deal of stress, which I had to overcome and control.

If you want to get your show on the road, you're going to have to learn how to cope with the stress of rapid, unpredictable movement; learn how to harness your energy; and control your anxieties as you strike out for the summit. The following test will help you assess your capacity to cope with this type of pressure and will show you how to strengthen these abilities:

1. What would you have to give up if you wanted to embark on a major life change that would bring success?:

   (a) _____

   (b) _____

   (c) _____

   (d) _____

2. What are your greatest fears associated with each loss?:

   (a) _____

   (b) _____

   (c) _____

   (d) _____

3. What's the worst thing that could happen if each of these fears was realized?:

(a) _____

(b) _____

(c) _____

(d) _____

4. How would you recover from each of these calamities?:

(a) _____

(b) _____

(c) _____

(d) _____

5. In each case, did your recovery depend on your own strength, or the help of someone else?:

My Strength to Cope   *The Person Who Would Help Out*

(a) _____   (a) _____

(b) _____   (b) _____

(c) _____   (c) _____

(d) _____   (d) _____

6. List six disasters you have had to deal with in your personal life or career:

(a) _____

(b) _____

(c) _____

(d) _____

(e) _____

(f) _____

7. What was the main lesson learned from each?:

(a) _____

(b) _____

(c) _____

(d) _____

(e) _____

(f) _____

8. What fail-safe techniques did you employ to ensure that you would not have to repeat these disasters?

(a) _____

(b) _____

(c) _____

(d) _____

(e) _____

(f) _____

9. If you failed to learn from each of these past disasters and take effective preventive action, will you do so now? Will you do so in the future when trouble strikes?

10. In analyzing your past failures, what were your chief emotional reactions to each?

☐ Self-doubt
☐ Anger
☐ Tendency to blame others
☐ Bulldog determination to find a way to prevail

The only healthy reaction is the last one. Self-doubt has no place in the mind of a winner. You need to count on yourself for the rest of your life. Wallowing in self-criticism will only injure your confidence. It won't add one grain of ability to your repertoire. Cut out the wallowing after a failure and learn what skills need strengthening in order to avoid future reverses. Then try again.

Anger is unharnessed energy. As such, it only depletes your capacities to succeed. If you need to feel angry, make sure that each wave of emotion leads to a productive bottom line—that burst of energy must be harnessed to produce something tangible of benefit to you; otherwise, it is entirely wasted. Energy conservation is a good policy, even with angry energy.

Blaming others puts control in their hands. If you've failed in some endeavor, even if someone else had a hand in it, don't waste time blaming the enemy. Find out, instead, what you could have done to attain greater control of the situation, so the next time nobody else will be able to thwart you.

Parlaying Your Success

I've learned that the best tactic for ensuring continued success and survival is to parlay one win into many others. That way, one failure won't set you back. Since some failures are inevitable, by cloning your successes, you are assured that some will survive.

When I had made it at "American Bandstand," I parlayed that success into my company, Dick Clark Productions. That move enabled me to diversify my sources of strength, so that when disaster struck and I lost my "Variety Show," I had many other avenues of success to pursue. You must have multiple channels for your success, as well. Take the following test to learn in which ways you can parlay your current success into a durable, winning career:

1. List the skills you possess which could be the basis for a higher degree of success than you now enjoy:

    (a) _____

    (b) _____

    (c) _____

    (d) _____

2. Do you get paid enough for your skills?

    Yes ☐   No ☐

    If no, is it because:

    (a) people are not aware of how valuable you are?
    (b) you are too shy to ask for more compensation, even though you deserve it?
    (c) you have been denied a more substantial reward and are afraid to leave the security of your current spot in order to get ahead?

(d) you feel that your worth will eventually be recognized if you give the situation more time?

If you answeres "Yes" to any of these possibilities, you have a serious problem in your ability to market your skills. Apparently, you realize how much you're worth, but others don't. Or they simply refuse to reward you appropriately. The solution to this problem is in marketing. Selling yourself (don't be shy to do this) is essential to achieving success.

Some people equate selling themselves with prostitution. It couldn't be further from the truth. To make your assets more visible means that they are likely to be more widely used, enjoyed, and relied upon. That increases the likelihood that you will be paid more for your skills and will be in a better bargaining position in general in your career. The key to selling yourself is making your skills essential to others so that they are willing to pay you what you deserve.

3. Define three variations on your career theme that could increase your level of success (new businesses, sidelines, consulting, etc.):

(a) _____

(b) _____

(c) _____

4. Which of these would be the easiest to accomplish right now?
5. Why haven't you already done so? Will you start today to diversify your success in order to ensure your survival?

In my life, I have suffered many reverses along with my big successes. In fact, it's hard for me to think of an umblemished success in my life. But, each time I was in danger, my ability to refer back to my life plan for guidance, deal with anxiety and uncertainty, and keep multiple success options open simultaneously enabled me to survive and thrive. In your life, try to define your goals via reviving your dreams; then learn to deal with your fears; and, with bulldog determination, parlay your successes into a durable winning streak.

EXERCISES FOR CHAPTER 3

How to Take Charge of Your Life

Getting on Top of the Problem

Each morning as you drive to work, I'm sure you appreciate the helicopter traffic reports given courtesy of your local radio station. I'll bet you also wish, at times, that you owned a helicopter yourself. That way, you wouldn't have to fight the slow-moving traffic. When it comes to surviving in life, you have to own a helicopter—not a mechanical one, but a mental one.

In order to conduct your life with authority, you must train yourself to scout ahead of where you are—as does the traffic helicopter—and get a broad picture of the situations you are embedded in. On the ground, you are too close to the action to get a clear, overall picture. In your life, you are too involved with day-to-day problems to take the helicopter view which could tell you that, although things are going smoothly at the moment, you ought to take a preventive detour because trouble lies ahead.

To survive, you have to become your own helicopter scout. You must learn to remove yourself from the immediate situation, from time to time, and look at the broad patterns of your life. In the following test, you will be given some help in achieving that perspective. Winners are people who pay attention to the minute detail of every vital situation. But they always seem to know which details need attention and which can be ignored for the moment. They accomplish this selection by taking the helicopter view, scouting ahead, and defining what their priorities should be.

1. In this exercise, you are being asked to prepare for a trip to Miami (or to New York, if you live in Miami). Scan *The New York Times* weather map and, in ten seconds, decide what to wear.

How well did you do? Were you able to go right to the appropriate forecast after scanning the overview? Or did you get lost in the detail right from the start and fail to find the information you were seeking in the allotted time?

You must train yourself to be a scout, take a quick survey of the overall territory, and find the key detail you need to make important decisions.

2. If weather charts make you dizzy, try this exercise to train your abilities to take the helicopter view of a situation:

Marie was tall, blonde, and very beautiful. She had a magnetism that could make even the most resolutely faithful man want to have an affair "just this one time." That afternoon, she had been at Dr. Petrocelli's office for a check-up. After telling her about the lump in her breast, he had proposed that they both "forget the doctor-patient relationship and go out for dinner."

At home that night, Marie felt an overwhelming need to confess to her husband, Jeff. "What would you do if you found out that I was attracted to another man?" she asked.

"That would depend on the circumstances, your actions, and my state of mind at the time," Jeff replied, not taking her query too seriously.

Indignant, Marie opened up and unloaded the bomb-shell. "I went out for dinner with another man tonight, Jeff. I wasn't working late at the office as I had said."

"What do you want me to say about that? 'Hooray'? Or: 'How could you do something like that to a decent guy like me?' I don't know what you want me to do about that information, Marie."

"Well, dammit, don't just accept it. I can't tolerate your passivity anymore. Maybe that's why I did what I did tonight. Maybe I just wanted to jolt you out of your inertia."

"Are we back to that issue again? Are you going to keep harping on the fact that I don't know what to do about my career, that I'm not the wage-earner you thought you were marrying?"

Marie fumed at Jeff's accusation that she was being mercenary. "You myopic bastard! You can't even tell when someone is on your side. I don't know what I'm going to do about you and our marriage."

"Neither do I," said Jeff, as he picked up his jacket and left the apartment.

Now it's time to take some action based on the story you have just read. If you are a woman, decide which of the suggested actions Marie should take. If you are a man, decide which of the following actions Jeff should take. Remember, only one top priority can exist at any one time. So you must decide what the very next step should be for Jeff and Marie:

Marie's Choices	Jeff's Choices
(a) See a lawyer.	(a) See a lawyer.
(b) Discuss the marital problem with a marriage counselor.	(b) Discuss the marital problem with a marriage counselor.
(c) Ask the advice of a best friend about what to do next.	(c) Ask the advice of a best friend about what to do next.
(d) See another doctor.	(d) Seek another job.
(e) Talk over the situation with your spouse	(e) Talk over the situation with your spouse.
(f) Give up on Jeff as a lost cause and start to date other men.	(f) Pay Marie back for what she did by having an affair.

Based on the information each of them had available at the time, there was only one *best* thing each of them could do:

Marie should have immediately consulted another doctor. Her physical examination had revealed a lump in her breast (had you forgotten about that?). Based on the fact that Marie and Dr. Petrocelli had abandoned the doctor-patient relationship, Marie's first priority should have been to consult another doctor right away.

Jeff, not knowing about the results of the examination, could not have had the same priority. For him, his marriage was clearly in crisis. Marie had stated that "he didn't know when someone [she] was on his side." That meant she still valued and wanted to maintain their relationship. Her action of dating another man was merely an attempt to provoke his jealously and get his attention. His first priority should have been to give her the attention she was seeking.

Most of life occurs as in the above story. There are lots of confusing things happening all at once. Intense emotions are provoked and they distract you from the right priorities. Only by taking the helicopter view—stepping back and saying, "Whoa . . . what's going on here. . . ? What's really most important *right now?*"—can you make the right decisions and pay attention to the most important priority *in detail.*

Taking Responsibility

I often hear business people make the following statement: "I'm going to delegate this responsibility to you. I want you to measure up. Don't disappoint me."

If you are that business person, you are deluding yourself. If you are the person to whom the assignment was made, you are taking on a task that is impossible to fulfill.

- *Responsibility* can never be delegated!
- *Authority* can be delegated.

As the person in charge of an overall project or business, you can never give away any portion of the responsibility to anyone, no matter how competent he or she is. If a mistake is made and the deal loses money, who pays? You do, of course. It's your business, and so you must pay for the mistakes of others. You always pay for everyone's mistakes at the bottom line. Hence, you, as boss, are always fully responsible. But, what you can do is to assign aspects of the task to other people—giving them authority to act on your behalf—as long as you clearly recognize your continuing responsibility for the overall success or failure of the enterprise.

If you work for someone, he or she may say that you are being given responsibility for a task, but it is really authority you are being handed. And that authority may have *hidden limits!* You ought to know the extent of the authority you wield: otherwise, you may find yourself in an embarrassing position when you are overruled by the boss. Since your supervisor has responsibility for everything under his or her span of control, your authority to do anything is always *temporary* and *limited.*

To maintain good relationships between workmates, you should always know what authority is being given, to whom, and for what time period. The following exercise will help you define the limits of authority within which you work:

1. List your most important duties (remember to include only those for which you have complete authority and responsibility):

    (a) _____

    (b) _____

    (c) _____

    (d) _____

2. To whom do you report on each of these responsibilities?:

    (a) _____

    (b) _____

    (c) _____

    (d) _____

3. Can your decision be overruled in any of these domains?

    Yes ☐   No ☐

If "Yes," then you have authority, *not* responsibility, in this task.

There is only one type of responsibility—that is where you have *total control* over a situation and you are directly affected by the bottom-line result.

4. In the sphere of authority, you may have one of three types:

   (a) *Observer Status*—you may be asked to represent your boss at a meeting and report back. But you are not given the power to act on his or her behalf.
   (b) *Instructed Delegate Status*—you are asked to represent your boss in a situation where you have clearly delimited powers. "You can buy the machine if the supplier offers less than $4,000. Try to make the best deal you can under that price," says your boss. Under those conditions, you are your boss's instructed delegate.
   (c) *Plenipotentiary Status*—your boss gives you power-of-attorney authority to act on his or her behalf. You can commit the boss to any price for that machine. The boss has no immediate recourse on that deal. But you can, and usually will, be fired for a gross misuse of this power-of-attorney authority.

In analyzing your most important duties in life (those which you listed in Question #1), which ones do you have complete responsibility over? And for which do you have one of these three types of authority?

MY MOST IMPORTANT DUTIES	OBSERVER STATUS	INSTRUCTED DELEGATE	POWER-OF-ATTORNEY AUTHORITY	COMPLETE RESPONSIBILITY
(a)				
(b)				
(c)				
(d)				

Next time you feel you are truly in charge of your life (or would like to be in that position), ask yourself, "Am I just too close to the situation to really know what's going on? Is it time for a helicopter ride to get a fresh view of where I stand?" In my own case, I do this very frequently. Every project in which I am involved is absorbing. It would be easy just to plod ahead, lost in the traffic of my burdens, forgetting my overall direction.

I take a mental helicopter ride every few months and review where my life and my career are heading. Then I make the necessary changes in direction. I have never yet gotten trapped in a dead end, despite all my life and career crises, because I am always able to get away from myself, look at my situation from far above, and see the jams before I get stuck in any. Or, if trapped in one, my mental helicopter tells me which detour will get me out of the trap most quickly.

In working with other people, I make it a point to know the power aspects of our relationship. I never act until I know what power I have. It would be a colossal waste of my energy to go off and prepare a large project unless I knew that I had the necessary power to defend it and make it work. The biggest mistake in my life—one which taught me a vital lesson—was when I worked so hard on the "Variety Show" only to see it get killed because I couldn't get it played in a prime-time weekend slot. I was so emotionally involved that I lost my perspective for a while. I should have realized that, although I had authority to produce the show, the power to run it in a given time slot wasn't mine. Each time I take on a project, I make certain to know the limits of my power and authority. If I haven't enough clout to ensure something will succeed, I ask for, or fight for, that power; otherwise, my efforts will be wasted. In your life, the best way to ensure your survival is to acquire the strength to implement and defend your decisions. You must have power in order to be in charge. That's a basic fact—one you can't escape. Be in charge of your life and get used to asking questions about and fighting for power.

EXERCISES FOR
CHAPTER 4

How to Build a
Winning Team

Building Trust

Lately we have been treated to a barrage of ads for American Express, which begin, "Do you know me? I climbed Mount Everest . . . I won the Masters Golf Tournament three times . . . etc." It's an appealing ad, but I think it glorifies the wrong heroes.

The people who should really be featured in these promotions are the truly anonymous people behind the scenes. I'd like to see some celebrity status given to Sir Edmund Hillary's Sherpa guide, the person who deserves at least half the credit for that successful climb. What about Jack Nicklaus's caddy, or Jim Fixx's editor—they are the vital people on the team who helped give these not-too-anonymous celebrities their successes.

Nobody can be a winner alone. It takes a team effort to make it to the top and to remain there. You must know how to build a winning team if you want to succeed and survive. Behind your achievements there will be many unsung heroes. You have to learn how to win their allegiance and their trust. In the following test, you will have an opportunity to check out your abilities to capture people's energies and mount a team effort to propel all of you to the top:

1. If you had to choose one sentence to define your goals—a sort of personal slogan that captures the essence of your mission in life—what would it be? Write it down below.

_____

_____

2. List the people in your life whom you consider most essential to your success:

(a) _____

(b) _____

(c) _____

(d) _____

(e) _____

(f) _____

(g) _____

(h) _____

(i) _____

(j) _____

3. Of these ten essential people, how many would recognize, as your personal code, the sentence you wrote in answer to Question #1?

4. Review the list of people you wrote down in answer to Question #2. Do you know the life goals of each?

Yes ☐   No ☐

If "No," then you will find it difficult to win this person's long-term allegiance. Unless you know what someone wants out of life, it will be impossible to help that person attain his or her goals. People will be loyal members of your team only if you are a key member of theirs. They want to get to the top. They have a right to aspire to success. You have to know their goals so that you can help them get where they are going. If someone recognizes that their destiny and yours are closely linked, they will fight like hell to push your career forward. If you don't make it, neither will they.

My career has been based on making other people into stars. Their successes have been the fuel for mine. As long as my associates continue to win through their alliance with me, my vehicle for victory will never run out of gas.

Helping People Grow

How many times have you gotten a frank, painful piece of advice or criticism from a well-meaning friend? Did you feel thankful for that person's efforts? If you are like most people, you will have nodded politely and then vowed to avoid that person for a while. Who wants to be put down, even if it's done politely and for your own good?

The sign of a true friend is the person who "tells you what you need to hear, not what you want to hear," and also helps you deal with the advice he or she has just given. There's a world of difference between someone who says, "That dress looks terrible on you," and a person who will follow up with, "I think you look more attractive in a high-waisted dress. Can I help you pick one out?"

Giving advice to friends and associates is not enough. The hallmark of a true friend is the follow-up effort to help them grow from the advice given.

In order to build a winning team, you have to assist many people's growth process. That means you have to make many unpopular statements about those closest to you; then, you have to follow up with assistance for the person to whom you have just handed a load of "constructive criticism."

1. List the most important people in your life. Next to each, write down their most serious, *correctable* weakness:

               Person   Correctable Fault

(a) _____

(b) _____

(c) _____

(d) _____

(e) _____

(f) _____

(g) _____

(h) _____

(i) _____

(j) _____

2. When was the last time you discussed these faults with that person?

3. If you haven't yet done so, will you now discuss that person's fault(s) and help him or her grow as a result?

Getting Out the Vote

As a person who relies on other people's help to attain your success, you must have constant support from the key people in your life. Politicians have learned that it is fatal to forget about their constituents right after they elect them to office. You have to constantly enlist people's support, especially at times of crisis. You have to be conscious of the need to renew your mandate—otherwise, there will be serious defections from the ranks, or even sabotage. People who are led need to feel involved in the leadership process. They have to know that they will be taken into your confidence when the chips are down, rather than be blindly and unwillingly led into battle. In other words, any leader (not just of the political variety) must constantly be running for office. You must never take the loyalty of your followers for granted. In the following test, you will learn how to renew the loyalty of your team and keep them working toward the common goal—mutual success:

1. List the major crises in your career:

   (a) _____

   (b) _____

   (c) _____

2. In each case, did you describe the problem in detail to the following people and ask for their support?

Crisis	Mate	Boss	Key Subordinate	Best Friend
(a)	☐	☐	☐	☐
(b)	☐	☐	☐	☐
(c)	☐	☐	☐	☐

3. What kept you from discussing the problem with each of these people?

4. Could you discuss your reluctance to talk about your problems with each of those key people, now that the crisis has passed?

Yes ☐   No ☐

   If "No," then you will be in danger of facing another crisis without being able to have the assistance of all the key people on your team. It would be wise to analyze your relationship with each of these critical individuals to detect and remedy the flaws in your relationship that keep you from calling for their support at critical turning points.

5. Of those people listed above, which of them calls on you for help regularly in times of crisis?

   ☐ Mate
   ☐ Boss
   ☐ Key Subordinate
   ☐ Best Friend

6. Have you asked each person whose name you didn't check off in Question #5 why they don't ask for your help at critical times?

Yes ☐   No ☐

   If "No," why not do so at the earliest possible time? Many people assume that you're too busy or important to bother with their problems. They suffer in silence, assuming that you consider their problems trivial. Then, when you're in trouble and need their help, they hold back in retaliation for an innocent act of omission on your part which their inferiority feelings or shyness helped to bring about.

You have to be aggressive in letting people know you are on their side. You must advertise that fact so widely that even your most timid associates will feel comfortable calling for your assistance.

If you want to build a winning team, you must build trust among your associates, giving them credit, even though you have the power to hog the limelight. They must always know your goals and be asked to support them. You must know their aspirations and offer advice and growing-promoting help for them to achieve success. You must never take for granted their support, but must, instead, constantly renew your mandate to lead them.

They, in turn, must always know that you stand ready to help them, even if they are shy and feel unimportant by comparison to you.

Winning is a team effort. My life is proof of that. You must learn how to captain the winning team; you can't play and win alone.

EXERCISES FOR
CHAPTER 5

How to Make It Big

Making the Whole Greater Than the Sum of the Parts

The world seems to be such a complex place; yet our minds, in an attempt to bring clarity out of this confusion, seem addicted to simple definitions:

- Are you a person who leaves toilet seats up or down?
- Do you install the roll of toilet tissue with the end on top or underneath?
- Do you like to lump things together or to break them down into smaller categories?
- Are you a regular or Sicilian pizza eater?
- Where do you stand when the Chinese food arrives: on the side of spicy, or sweet and sour?

Wars have been fought to determine the superiority of one philosophy over another, as if this world were made up of an infinite variety of competing species, rather than being a place where all people share common emotions, needs, and fears. In order to make it big in this world, you have to be a person who can see beyond the differences in people and identify the elements which unite them. Being able to zero in on universals enables you to find wide markets for your ideas and products. And that ability is what separates those who make it big from all the rest.

I have always been presumptuous enough to believe that what I like and how I feel are not too different from anyone else's preferences and emotions. Hence, by tuning in to myself, I open the doors to those "universal truths." Before I do anything for anyone else, I first have to like it instinctively. After subjecting any new idea to this "gut reaction," I submit it to a careful analysis to determine its realistic feasibility. In essence, every project to which I commit myself has to pass two tests:

1. The test of the heart
2. The test of the mind

If you want to make it big, you have to learn how to employ both faculties to their greatest advantage. In our age of specialization, with computers at our disposal and endless parades of consultants at our beck and call, it has fallen out of fashion to use these native abilities. "Just put it through the computer and we'll get some projections as to the feasibility of the deal," says a business person, abdicating his or her responsibility to use God-given attributes that are far more accurate than any computer. The following exercises will help you revive and massage both aspects of your capabilities—the rational and the emotional:

1. Read the following descriptions and decide which of them more accurately describes your attitudes and your behavior:

Group A	Group B
• I like to play by the rules.	• I love to find new ways to play the game.
• Emotions should be controlled.	• Emotions should be shared.
• I believe it is my duty to protect others.	• I seek shelter in groups.
• I hate dreamers.	• I love getting into my own head.
• I love action.	• I get uptight with too much aggression.
• Detail is all-important.	• The overall picture is the vital thing; detail is relatively unimportant.
• I do things, one by one, in an organized way.	• I skip around from one thing to another, depending on what I think is important at the time.

2. Do you belong to Group A or Group B? The people who are Group A types tend to be better at administration. Those who fall into the B category are usually the more creative people. In order to be a big winner, you must be *both* a good administrator and creative in everything you do. If you belong to Group A, you ought to try the exercises listed below to stimulate your creativity. For a Group B creative person, you need to balance out your personality with a little good old-fashioned discipline:

EXERCISE FOR A GROUP A PERSON
1. Relax.
2. Close your eyes.
3. Breathe in and out, taking four seconds for each inhalation and exhalation. Count as you breathe:

> one . . . two . . . three . . . four . . . EXHALE
> one . . . two . . . three . . . four . . . INHALE

4. As you breathe in this relaxed fashion, let your mind do a survey of all the muscles in your body, starting from your forehead . . . to your scalp . . . to your neck, shoulders, and jaw . . . to your chest muscles . . . to your abdomen . . . to your back . . . to your rectum and pelvic area . . . to your thighs and calves . . . down to the tips of your toes.

   As you scan through these muscles groups, first tense them up so that you really feel their maximum tension; then fully relax each muscle group, one by one, until all your muscles are relaxed. Keep breathing in and out slowly while you completely relax all your muscles. The only movement in your body should be the rhythmic, gentle heaving of your abdomen as you breathe.

   After ten or twenty minutes, your mind will gradually relax and unwind, preparing you for creative thinking.

5. As you lie there in total relaxation, take one problem you have had in your life and just hold it in your consciousness. Don't try to solve it. Just keep the problem in your mind as you continue to breathe slowly and relax your muscles.

   Pretty soon, you will notice your mind begins to register apparently irrelevant information and images. Don't evaluate the flow of ideas; just continue to relax and center your mind on your problem in a calm, mental atmosphere.

6. As your mind gives you new images and information, be receptive and make a mental note of each thought. Don't agonize over whether or not you will remember them.

7. After about twenty minutes, sit up and tackle the problem from a rational point of view. You will probably find that this exercise has liberated new options for you to consider, creative channels that could only be opened through relaxed, free association.

8. Do this exercise each day until it becomes second nature to use your creativity as much as you use your analytical faculties to solve problems.

EXERCISE FOR A GROUP B PERSON

1. Draw up a list of all the most important priorities in your life (in order of importance):

(a) _____

(b) _____

(c) _____

(d) _____

(e) _____

(f) _____

(g) _____

(h) _____

(i) _____

(j) _____

2. For each of these, indicate whether you feel inspired to tackle it in the near future, or whether you feel apathetic and ambivalent:

Priority	Inspired	Apathetic / Ambivalent
(a)	☐	☐
(b)	☐	☐
(c)	☐	☐
(d)	☐	☐
(e)	☐	☐
(f)	☐	☐
(g)	☐	☐
(h)	☐	☐
(i)	☐	☐
(j)	☐	☐

3. Now re-arrange your priority list, placing at the top those tasks for which you are apathetic and/or ambivalent. Those tasks which inspire you, place on the list below all the ones which don't turn you on.

4. Now, examine the new list of priorities. It has, at the top, the tasks that are necessary but dull. You need to do them first. Your nature makes you avoid drudgery even when its necessary and must be gotten out of the way. If you follow the practice outlined above, your creative nature will soon be complemented by a disciplined, administrative way of coping with problems. You need both creativity and discipline to be a winner.

Contact . . . Impact

Any time you try to achieve something that you hope will find favor with a wide audience, be they paying customers or your friends and family, you need to ask yourself the following questions.

- Am I reaching them?
- What's the impact of my message on them?

All too often, people pay attention to only one of these factors and disregard the other with disastrous effects. If your friend is ignoring you, you'll surely reach him or her with a remark such as "Your wife/husband really is terrific in bed." Contact will be achieved, but what about the impact? Or, someone may have a wonderful motive behind their actions and mean to deliver it to a wide group, but will fail to make contact. Such is the case with a person who wants to advocate love and equal justice for all, but does so while you are walking to work during rush hour, accosting you and handing you a pamphlet preaching universal love. Without the proper contact, there will be no impact.

In the following exercise, you will undergo a test of your ability to make contact and have the right impact on others:

Jean had just come home from a difficult day at work. When she arrived home, Bill was fuming.

"What the hell do you mean by spending this amount of money last month? Do you think we're the Rockefellers or Vanderbilts? Since you've gone to work, you think that your measly salary is a fortune and have gone hog-wild with your charge accounts."

"First of all, Bill, I don't think that I'm accountable to you on money to the extent that you demand. Your income is greater than mine, I'll admit that. But that isn't license for you to be the financial dictator around here."

"Well, then, let's get separate bank and charge accounts. If you go broke, that's your affair. I don't want to go down with your ship, Jean."

"What do we do about the kids' expenses? Do we split them 50/50, or according to our incomes?"

"Goddammit, Jean! The way you're talking reminds me of the way George Slater and Emily did, just before their divorce —who gets how much of whose salary, and for what:"

At that, Jean began to cry and then shouted self-righteously, "You bastard! The only reason the charge account bill was so high last month was that I bought you the set of golf clubs you've wanted for such a long time. I've kept them hidden until your birthday. I only bought them last month because they were on sale. Maybe I'll return them now. You don't deserve them."

"You're being real generous to me with my own money, Jean. Thanks, but, no, thanks."

"Fuck you, Bill. Why don't we get a divorce, like the Slaters. At least that way I'll have some peace of mind and control over my own life."

2. In this story, what are the messages the two people are trying to get across to each other:

	Bill	Jean
(a) Love	☐	☐
(b) Control	☐	☐
(c) Hate	☐	☐
(d) Devotion	☐	☐
(e) Responsibility	☐	☐
(f) Revenge	☐	☐
(g) Obedience	☐	☐

3. Of the many possibilities (assuming this couple really loves each other and would like to stay together), which emotion and lessons should they be trying to convey most?

4. Write a brief statement that each of them should make to each other to convey the really vital message that you have identified in Question #3. Practice your hand at being a script writer. In your own communicating, make your statements have both these essential qualities:

- The ability to make the right kind of contact
- The proper impact on the other person

Making it big means being the person who is creative enough to find unique solutions; being a hard-nosed administrator who can bring a dream to fruition; and making your creation have the right impact on the right people, at the proper time, and in the best way. You are judged in heaven for your spirit. On earth, your deeds determine the reception you'll get from your audience, your business associates, your friends, and your family.

EXERCISES FOR
CHAPTER 6

How to Bounce Back from Failure

Don't Use Your Head as a Battering Ram

Failure is a bitter pill to swallow, even once. That's why we usually like to get away from it as quickly as possible. I feel that way, too, except that I've learned to hang around my defeats just long enough to analyze what went wrong so that I'll never have to face the same result a second time.

How do you handle defeats? Have you learned important lessons from them, or have you persisted doggedly along the same pathways, never learning from failures, destined to relive them many times over?

In the following exercise, you'll analyze the results of past failures—what you did or didn't gain from them. Your head is a delicate and sophisticated tool. Don't use it as a battering ram. Don't attack life from one unchanging angle, never being informed by your failures:

1. List the major failures in your life:

    (a) _____

    (b) _____

    (c) _____

    (d) _____

    (e) _____

2. What vital lesson did you learn from each? What was responsible for the occurrence?:

    (a) _____

    (b) _____

    (c) _____

    (d) _____

    (e) _____

3. Cite a subsequent experience in which you put this important lesson to work with better results:

    (a) _____

    (b) _____

    (c) _____

    (d) _____

    (e) _____

4. List the five most important people in your life:

(a) _____

(b) _____

(c) _____

(d) _____

(e) _____

5. What important need of yours does each person satisfy?:

(a) _____

(b) _____

(c) _____

(d) _____

(e) _____

6. To whom else would you turn in order to satisfy this need if the primary person stopped giving you this gratification?:

(a) _____

(b) _____

(c) _____

(d) _____

(e) _____

7. List the most important priorities in your life:

(a) _____

(b) _____

(c) _____

(d) _____

(e) _____

8. Which of these has been re-examined in the past six months?

9. Which of these could be discarded if the need arose?

10. Of the priorities listed in answer to Question #7, which ones can be worked on most effectively right now, and which ones will take a while to get under way?

Priority	I can do something about this right now	I'll have to wait to get this under way
(a)	☐	☐
(b)	☐	☐
(c)	☐	☐
(d)	☐	☐
(e)	☐	☐

11. Are you working on useful priorities that can be accomplished right now? Or are you wasting lots of time ruminating over things that lie off in the distant future? If the latter is true, re-arrange your priorities to put first those tasks that will yield success in the here-and-now.

12. Add up the following numbers without the use of pencil and paper:

$$
\begin{array}{r}
346 \\
298 \\
346 \\
360 \\
457 \\
968 \\
297 \\
336 \\
\hline
\end{array}
$$

13. What total did you get? Did you get confused, trying to keep all those numbers in your head at one time? There was really no need for that. You could have used a calculator. All I said was, "Don't use pencil and paper." You took that to mean that you had to do things the hard way. So did most other people. My instruction could just as easily have implied that there is any easy way out—a calculator.

Most people get trapped by their own feelings of guilt. They feel that doing things the easy way is cheating. Instead, they choose the hardest way out—a philosophy sure to lead to a lot of failure.

14. With your trusty calculator in hand, multiply the following figures:

    99632 times 77456 = ?

15. What is the correct answer?

16. How many times did you repeat this calculation before you finally believed the calculator rather than this book? Most hand-held calculators can't do this multiplication. There are too many numbers to handle, and so the little brain flashes its signal for "overflow condition." Yet, you continued on, not learning from the failure—insistent that "if Dick Clark says

you can multiply these two numbers together, he must be right." Dick Clark can be wrong! He's been wrong many times before. Trust your own experience, not the commands given in any book. Learn primarily from observing life. Don't be swayed by the influences around you to an extent that you fail to trust your own experience.

Make Mid-Course Corrections

After you have launched any project, you can count on the fact that there will be many detours and adjustments required before you get to your goal. How adaptable are you? How well do you make mid-course corrections? Your ability to bounce back from failure will be largely determined by your capacity to shift gears at the appropriate time and place.

1. Name your most important goal in life:

2. What skills are necessary for you to achieve that goal?:

   (a) _____

   (b) _____

   (c) _____

   (d) _____

   (e) _____

3. Do you possess all of the necessary skills?

      Yes ☐   No ☐

   If "No," what are you doing now to acquire these missing skills?

4. If one or more of these skills couldn't be attained, how would you compensate for it in order to be able to reach your goal in spite of that deficit? List one alternate strategy to get around the lack of each vital skill:

(a) _____

(b) _____

(c) _____

(d) _____

(e) _____

5. Don't you think it would be wise to develop and refine this alternate capacity, just in case?

6. Discover the key to the following number sequence:

$$1, 3, 5, 7, 9, 10, 12, 15, 19, 24$$

7. How'd you do? It's a bit confusing. That's because I changed rules on you in midstream. At first, I gave you numbers that differed by 2. Then, after 9, I used widening intervals: 1, 2, 3, 4, 5.

I never promised you that I would keep the same rule all through the sequence. Life will never make or keep such a promise to you, either. You'll find that the rules of the game keep changing. Your job is to notice when the rules shift and make adjustments accordingly—make mid-course corrections.

8. Discover the key to the following sequence:

$$2, 9, 5, 35, 67, 126, 2398$$

9. What was your answer? A bit tricky, this example, huh? That's because it obviously follows no sequence at all. I just picked out numbers at random. As in the previous example, where the calculator couldn't compute the answer, did you believe your experience, or this book? When are you going to learn to trust your own experience and judgment? Just because Dick Clark says, "Discover the key to the following sequence," doesn't mean that it can be done. Sometimes the rule you discover is that *"the problem can't be solved."* If that's the case, then make a mid-course correction—stop wasting your time on it—and go on to something more productive.

Learning from Failure

1. In doing all the previous exercises, where did you go off track?:

(a) _____

(b) _____

(c) _____

(d) _____

(e) _____

2. Were you able to remember the instances where you failed?

Yes ☐   No ☐

If "No," then you are still in the habit of rushing right past your failures without learning anything from them. To avoid defeat in the future, learn a lesson from defeats in the present.

As you recall the episodes in my life, I'm sure you'll agree that I have come a long way on the road to success, and also that I've had my share of failures. In my opinion, success and failure are two sides of the same coin. The loftier your goals, the more severe will be the failures to which you're exposed. Some people stop at that point and say, "I can't deal with big losses. I guess I'll lower my sights." That's a pity, since after each loss, you've learned so much that it's likely your next try will succeed. Use a failure as a lesson for growth. Since you've already paid your dues with the frustration of defeat, why not cash in on the benefits that defeat can yield —enhanced experience and growth? Another important point about failure is that, once you've experienced it, you can say, "Heck, if I survived this one and then bounced back, I'm not so afraid of defeat anymore. I'll always figure out a way to get up off the floor and get back in the game."

My life has been as full of big victories as anyone's. I attribute my successes more to the ability to bounce back from defeat than to the talent that got me to the top in the first place.